My Life Manual

Estate Planning,
Information and Messages for your Executors
and Loved Ones

HM Todd

Copyright © 2016 Hazel Todd
All rights reserved.

ISBN -10: 0-9944978-2-2

ISBN-13: 978-0-9944978-2-6

This work is copyright. All works reserved by the publisher. Apart from any use as permitted by law, no part of this publication may be reproduced, stored in a retrieval system, or transmitted in any form or by any means, electronic, digital, mechanical, photocopying, recorded or otherwise, without the prior written permission of the copyright owner. Requests and queries concerning reproduction an rights may be addressed to :

The Publisher
PO Box 167
Balwyn North
Victoria
3104
Australia.

www.the-life-manual.com

DISCLAIMER

The material in this publication is of the nature of general comment only, and it does not represent professional, legal or financial advice. It is not intended to provide specific guidance for particular circumstances and it should not be relied upon as the basis for any decision to take action or not to take action on any matter covered in this book. Readers should obtain professional advice where appropriate and before making any decisions on the basis of the contents of this book. To the maximum extent permitted by law, the author and publisher disclaim all responsibility and liability to any person arising directly or indirectly from any person taking or not taking action based on the information in this publication.

Edited by: Sue Braint
Cover by: Raffy Hoylar

DEDICATION

For my Dad

Contents

IMPORTANT NOTICE TO ALL READERS 1
   Tips to Update and Protect Valuable Information 2
   Protection of Valuable Information 2
   Who Should Use This Manual? 2
   Checklist to Review your Estate Planning Options 3
WHO I AM 5
My Personal Details 5
   My Team of Professional Advisors 7
   Employment Details 9
   My Accounts and Subscriptions 10
   Loyalty Cards and Frequent Flyer Miles 11
   Personal and Important Documents 12
   My Online World 13
WHAT I'M WORTH 15
   Assets 15
      Real Estate 15
      Bank, Building Society or Credit Union Accounts 19
      Shares or Securities in Companies 20
      Managed Funds 21
      Units in Real Estate Investment Trust Funds 22
      Monetary Investment Details 23
      Motor Vehicles 24
      Private Companies and Businesses 26
      Online Assets 28
      Other Assets 29
   Superannuation and Trusts 30
      My Superannuation 30
      Superannuation Pensions 32
      My Pensions 32
      Powers of Attorney and the Withdrawal of Super before Death 33
      My Trust Interests 34
      Executorships 36
      Powers to Appoint 37

    Letter of Wishes to My Trustee 37
  Personal Items 38
    Sentimental Possessions 38
    My Personal Possessions 41
    Items in my Possession that Do Not Belong to Me 42
    Heirlooms 43
  Liabilities 44
    My Liabilities 44
    Secured Debts 44
    Unsecured Debts 46
    Guarantees 47
    Tax 48

PLANNING FOR THE ALL EVENTUALITIES *50*
  If I Become Incapacitated 50
  My Powers of Attorney 51
  My Living Will or Advanced Care Directive 54
  Insurance 55
    Life Insurance: 55
    Other Forms of Insurance 56
  Estate Planning and Asset Protection Instruments 58
  Trusts 58
    Implied Trusts 59
    Express Trusts 60
    Discretionary Trusts 62
    Life Interests 63
    Accommodation Fund Trust 65
    Right of Occupation and Use and Enjoyment Trusts 66
    Special Needs, Special Disability or Protective Trusts 67
    Children's Trusts 69
    Education Trusts 69
    Capital Reserve Trusts 70
    Testamentary Trusts 71
    Beneficiary Controlled Testamentary Trust 73
    Estate Proceeds Trust 74
  Superannuation 75
    Withdrawal of Super Funds 75
    Persons Eligible to receive your Superannuation Death Benefit 78
    Binding Death Benefit Nominations. 78
    Tax on Death Benefits 79

- Superannuation Death Benefits Testamentary Trust 80
- Superannuation Complaints Tribunal (SCT) 80

Caveats 81
Mortgages 81
Equitable Mortgages 81
Change in Title 82
Buy-Sell Agreements 83
Binding Financial Agreements 84
Interest Free Loans 85
Insolvency 86

WHEN I PASS AWAY 87

Organ Donation 87
Funeral Arrangements 89
- My Funeral Arrangements 89
- If I die overseas 90
- My Obituary 91
- My Eulogy 91
- Message to be Read at my Funeral 91
- Notifications 93

Last Will and Testament 95
- The Need for a Will 95
- When to Revise your Will 96
- Validity of a Will 98
- Things to Consider Before Making a Will 98
- Executors 102
- Challenges to a Will 108
- Measures of Protection to a Claim Against your Estate 109
- Long Term Relationships (not *De Facto*) 111
- Where to Store your Will 112
- Alterations to Your Will 113
- Mutual Wills 113
- International Will and Assets 114
- Revocation of a Will 114
- Deed of Family Arrangement 114
- Dying Without a Will 115
- My Will 116
- Notes on Why I Drafted my Will as I Did 116
- Further Notes on Why I Re-drafted my Will 118

- Probate Guide 120
  - Suggestions to Beneficiaries of my Estate on How to Manage Their Inheritance 122
- Others for Whom I Care 123
  - Pets 124
  - Charities I Support. 126

MESSAGES 127
- Letters to Loved Ones 127
- Letters for Forgiveness 129
- Letter to the Future Step-parent of my Children 130
- Guardians of my Children 131
- My Notes to my Guardians 133

TEMPLATES 136
- Will Kit 136
- Last Will And Testament 141
- Statutory Declaration Template 143

NOTES 146
FINAL WORD 147
ABOUT THE AUTHOR 148

1
IMPORTANT NOTICE TO ALL READERS

The contents of this book are for information purposes to help you keep track of your financial growth and plans and as an aid to your executors once you pass on.

Another purpose of this book is to comfort and assist those you leave behind in finalising your affairs, by giving them access to valuable information. The contents of this book are your final words on all the things that are important to you.

It is important that you leave this book in a safe place with your other important papers and documents so that your family can easily find it. It is suggested that you tell someone you trust that you have put together this information.

You should bear in mind that the contents of this manual could be used in evidence in the event of a challenge to your Will, estate or guardianship.

The contents of this book do not alter or supplement the contents of your Last Will and Testament, nor does it replace the need for a properly executed Will, nor legal or financial advice. It also does not stand in the place of a properly executed Enduring Power of Attorney should you become incapacitated and thus unable to deal with your affairs.

Any person reading the information provided in this book should note that it does not create any legal or equitable obligations to anyone and that the person who provided this information did so with this in mind. This information is for general assistance only.

Tips to Update and Protect Valuable Information

It is important that you keep this manual up to date. Update it after any significant life event, such as any births, deaths, marriages or divorces, or any other significant change of circumstances, particularly financial or health related.

Protection of Valuable Information

It is important to protect our most valuable assets and that includes information. Information such as account details and passwords are at risk of abuse in the wrong hands.

1. Ensure that you keep this manual somewhere safe, or even in a safe if you have access to one and away from prying eyes;
2. Do not include sensitive financial information;
3. It is important never to brag or be careless about disclosing the extent of your assets to others, particularly strangers;
4. Do not write down pin numbers or passwords, or if you do try to encode it in some way so that it is not obvious that it's a password or pin number;
5. Scam artists can be very creative in extracting personal information. Be on the alert for anything that just doesn't feel right. It is always acceptable to question those looking for information. Rather risk offending them, then being ripped off by them!

Who Should Use This Manual?

This manual is for anyone, parents, couples, singles, young or old, anyone who wishes to organise their affairs, both for themselves and their family left behind.

This book will provide you with an overview of your financial position. Are you meeting your goals? Are you where you want to be at this stage of your life financially? You will note the changes in your finances with time, as you periodically review this book.

The purpose of this book is to ease the burden on your loved ones in finalising your affairs, having all the information available so that your executors can do their job, while removing some stress for your family when you pass on.

Your executors need this information to administer your estate. If you have no family or your family may not be aware of the full extent of your financial position, your executors may have a hard time locating all of your assets and knowing how to wind up your affairs.

But also, how many times have you tried to have the conversation about what your family should do in the event of your death? They may have avoided the conversation, as if in doing so the unthinkable will not happen. Or if the conversation does take place they are often so preoccupied thinking about how they would deal with the loss that nothing is really heard or remembered.

Checklist to Review your Estate Planning Options

- Is your relationship status the same?
- Have there been any subsequent births, deaths or marriages in your family?
- Has any member of your family been declared bankrupt?
- Is the choice of the executor in your Will still appropriate?
- Is your choice of guardian still appropriate?
- Is the appointor of any trust still appropriate?
- Has your Binding Death Benefits Nomination (BDBN) been reviewed and updated within the last three years?
- Have you disposed of any asset that you specifically gifted in your Will?
- Have your acquired more property?
- Have the needs of any of your family members changed?
- Has your health changed?
- Are you starting to have problems with your memory?

Date this information was last reviewed

Date	Details of review	Reminder set for next review date*

You may wish to set a reminder in your diary or phone for when you next wish to review the information in this manual.

2
WHO I AM
My Personal Details

Surname: _____
Given names: _____
Maiden name (if appropriate): _____
Address: _____
Domicile (permanent place of residence): _____
Nationality: _____
Previous nationality: _____
Prior country of residence: _____
Date of birth: _____
Place of birth: _____
Other names or other spellings of names: _____

Note: If you have gone by other names in the past and in particular have any assets or obligations under that name, you should make a note of it in your Will. Therefore, the alternative name will appear on the grant of probate and your executor can easily deal with all of your assets. Alternatively, amend the ownership documentation now to reflect your full and correct name.

Making a note of your nationality or country of prior residence could be useful, having regard to any State pension entitlement from that country, or if there is a possibility that you have assets there.

You may also wish to keep a record of any changes in address, as your address will be an identifier to certain accounts and therefore relevant to your executor in locating your assets, such as lost Super.

Change of Address

Date of change: _____
New address: _____
_____

Date of change: _____
New address: _____
_____

Date of change: _____
New address: _____
_____

Date of change: _____
New address: _____
_____

Date of change: _____
New address: _____
_____

Date of change: _____
New address: _____
_____

Date of change: _____
New address: _____
_____

My Team of Professional Advisors

Keep a list of your go-to team so you know who to consult when an issue arises and to keep track of important documents belonging to you that they may have in their possession.

After you pass away your family and executor could have many questions, which your advisers can assist with as well as providing the your important documents, such as your Will, Certificate of Title or tax returns. These advisors could also assist with the winding up your affairs. Make a note of your various advisors or professionals, such as:

- Solicitor;
- Accountant;
- Tax advisor;
- Property advisor;
- Financial planner/advisor;
- Investment broker; etc.

Name of firm: _____
Contact person: _____ Profession: _____
Address of firm: _____
Telephone: _____ Email: _____
Documents belonging to me in their possession: _____
_____
Types of matters they have assisted me with: _____
_____
_____

Name of firm: _____
Contact person: _____ Profession: _____
Address of firm: _____
Telephone: _____ Email: _____
Documents belonging to me in their possession: _____
_____

Types of matters they have assisted me with: _____
_____
_____

Name of firm: _____
Contact person: _____ Profession: _____
Address of firm: _____
Telephone: _____ Email: _____
Documents belonging to me in their possession: _____
_____
Types of matters they have assisted me with: _____
_____
_____

Name of firm: _____
Contact person: _____ Profession: _____
Address of firm: _____
Telephone: _____ Email: _____
Documents belonging to me in their possession: _____
_____
Types of matters they have assisted me with: _____
_____
_____

Name of firm: _____
Contact person: _____ Profession: _____
Address of firm: _____
Telephone: _____ Email: _____
Documents belonging to me in their possession: _____
_____
Types of matters they have assisted me with: _____
_____
_____

Employment Details

Name of employer: _____
Address: _____
Date of employment: _____ Position: _____
Benefits/entitlements/notes: _____
_____
Termination reason: _____ Date: _____

Name of employer: _____
Address: _____
Date of employment: _____ Position: _____
Benefits/entitlements/notes: _____
_____
Termination reason: _____ Date: _____

Name of employer: _____
Address: _____
Date of employment: _____ Position: _____
Benefits/entitlements/notes: _____
_____
Termination reason: _____ Date: _____

Name of employer: _____
Address: _____
Date of employment: _____ Position: _____
Benefits/entitlements/notes: _____
_____
Termination reason: _____ Date: _____

My Accounts and Subscriptions

Supplier/provider: _____
Service or product provided: _____
Method of payment: _____ Account No.: _____

Supplier/provider: _____
Service or product provided: _____
Method of payment: _____ Account No.: _____

Supplier/provider: _____
Service or product provided: _____
Method of payment: _____ Account No.: _____

Supplier/provider: _____
Service or product provided: _____
Method of payment: _____ Account No.: _____

Supplier/provider: _____
Service or product provided: _____
Method of payment: _____ Account No.: _____

Supplier/provider: _____
Service or product provided: _____
Method of payment: _____ Account No.: _____

Supplier/provider: _____
Service or product provided: _____
Method of payment: _____ Account No.: _____

Supplier/provider: _____
Service or product provided: _____
Method of payment: _____ Account No.: _____

Loyalty Cards and Frequent Flyer Miles

Some people do not realise that many loyalty programs allow the members' loyalty points to be transferred on their death. And in some cases these can be of value, having accumulated over a significant period of time.

Loyalty program: _____
Account number: _____
Notes: _____
_____

Loyalty program: _____
Account number: _____
Notes: _____
_____

Loyalty program: _____
Account number: _____
Notes: _____
_____

Loyalty program: _____
Account number: _____
Notes: _____
_____

Loyalty program: _____
Account number: _____
Notes: _____
_____

Personal and Important Documents

In writing this list, you must ensure that your documents are secure and locked away, preferably in a fire proof safe, and that this information is not open to abuse or identity theft. It is also important to keep this book safe and away from those who may misuse this information.

These documents may be required to prove or defend a claim by your guardian, should you become incapacitated, or your executor in administering your estate.

My important documents are located as noted below:

Birth certificates: _____
Passports: _____
Citizenship certificates: _____
Certificates of Title: _____
Vehicle registration: _____
Insurance policies: _____
Tax returns and related information: _____
Immunisation certificates: _____
Documents relating to medical history: _____
Prescriptions: _____
Share Certificates: _____
Powers of Attorney: _____
Safety deposit box: _____
Storage unit: _____
Other: _____
_____
_____
_____
_____

My Online World

For some our digital online world can be of great value. In the event that any of your online accounts or assets are of worth, either sentimental or financial, you may wish to make specific provision for this in your Will. For example, for some people a blog is a lucrative business that could be sold or passed onto someone.

Likewise, if you become incapacitated, your appointed attorney or administrator may need to know these details so that your online presence can be managed. To access these accounts your executor would need to know the user names and passwords. Though oftentimes, as long as they have access to your email account, passwords can be reset and usernames provided. Some sites have security questions which would offer a level of protection for you, but difficulty for others.

Cyber law is a relatively new area of law, with the added complexity that it may be difficult to ascertain which law should apply, as you may reside in one country, have a website registered in another and have it hosted a third.

Each site will have varying rules as to ownership of the account and its contents, and as anyone who has ever operated any form of online account knows, the terms and conditions change constantly. Realistically I would doubt that anyone ever reads these conditions. Who knows what we could all be agreeing to, someone from Facebook could one day knock on your door and demand your left kidney that you apparently agreed to donate!

Some online account providers will not transfer an account due to privacy law considerations. And for this reason you too may prefer that your online presence passes away with you.

If anything should happen to you, your family may also be comforted by access to your Facebook or Instagram account, and in particular the digital images which belong to you.

I have the following online presence and accounts, be it Facebook, Instagram, Blogs, Email, Twitter, Tumblr, Pinterest, eBay, YouTube, or any other.

Account type: _____ Provider: _____
Username: _____
What should be done with them: _____
_____

Account type: _____ Provider: _____
Username: _____
What should be done with them: _____
_____

Account type: _____ Provider: _____
Username: _____
What should be done with them: _____
_____

Account type: _____ Provider: _____
Username: _____
What should be done with them: _____
_____

Account type: _____ Provider: _____
Username: _____
What should be done with them: _____
_____

Account type: _____ Provider: _____
Username: _____
What should be done with them: _____
_____

3

WHAT I'M WORTH

Assets

Real Estate

There are various tax implications depending on how and why you own the property, be it Capital Gains Tax (CGT) for investment properties, income tax and so on. Property is often a long term investment and therefore proper records should be kept.

Property 1

Owned solely/jointly with: _____
Address: _____
Location of title documents: _____
Mortgaged with: _____
Date purchased: _____ Date sold: _____
Conveyancer: _____
Location of receipts and documents relevant to CGT: _____
Rental agent: _____
Telephone: _____ Email: _____
Building permits issued: _____
Major repairs by: _____ Date: _____

Work done: _____
Major repairs by: _____ Date: _____
Work done: _____
Things to look out for: _____
_____
_____

Property 2

Owned solely/jointly with: _____
Address: _____
Location of title documents: _____
Mortgaged with: _____
Date purchased: _____ Date sold: _____
Conveyancer: _____
Location of receipts and documents relevant to CGT: _____
Rental agent: _____
Telephone: _____ Email: _____
Building permits issued: _____
Major repairs by: _____ Date: _____
Work done: _____
Major repairs by: _____ Date: _____
Work done: _____
Things to look out for: _____
_____
_____

Property 3

Owned solely/jointly with: _____
Address: _____
Location of title documents: _____
Mortgaged with: _____

Date purchased: _____ Date sold: _____
Conveyancer: _____
Location of receipts and documents relevant to CGT: _____
Rental agent: _____
Telephone: _____ Email: _____
Building permits issued: _____
Major repairs by: _____ Date: _____
Work done: _____
Major repairs by: _____ Date: _____
Work done: _____
Things to look out for: _____
_____
_____

Property 4

Owned solely/jointly with: _____
Address: _____
Location of title documents: _____
Mortgaged with: _____
Date purchased: _____ Date sold: _____
Conveyancer: _____
Location of receipts and documents relevant to CGT: _____
Rental agent: _____
Telephone: _____ Email: _____
Building permits issued: _____
Major repairs by: _____ Date: _____
Work done: _____
Major repairs by: _____ Date: _____
Work done: _____
Things to look out for: _____
_____
_____

Property 5

Owned solely/jointly with: _____

Address: _____

Location of title documents: _____

Mortgaged with: _____

Date purchased: _____ Date sold: _____

Conveyancer: _____

Location of receipts and documents relevant to CGT: _____

Rental agent: _____

Telephone: _____ Email: _____

Building permits issued: _____

Major repairs by: _____ Date: _____

Work done: _____

Major repairs by: _____ Date: _____

Work done: _____

Things to look out for: _____

_____

_____

Other Notes: _____

_____

_____

_____

_____

_____

_____

_____

_____

_____

_____

_____

Bank, Building Society or Credit Union Accounts

It may be relevant to keep a record of where money has come from and gone to, such as money received from an inheritance, which could be relevant to family law matters or so that your executor can locate your assets. If there is a dispute with your estate, this information could be important. You should also make note of any online accounts such as PayPal or bitcoins.

Name of financial institution: _____
Branch: _____
BSB number: _____ Account number: _____
Funds acquired from: _____
Date account closed: _____ Funds transferred to: _____

Name of financial institution: _____
Branch: _____
BSB number: _____ Account number: _____
Funds acquired from: _____
Date account closed: _____ Funds transferred to: _____

Name of financial institution: _____
Branch: _____
BSB number: _____ Account number: _____
Funds acquired from: _____
Date account closed: _____ Funds transferred to: _____

Name of financial institution: _____
Branch: _____
BSB number: _____ Account number: _____
Funds acquired from: _____
Date account closed: _____ Funds transferred to: _____

Shares or Securities in Companies

For holdings on the ASX CHESS Share Register, the details of my sponsoring broker are as follows:

Name: _____
Address: _____
Telephone: _____ Email: _____
Contact person: _____

Company: _____
Number of shares: _____ Type: _____
Date acquired: _____ Date sold: _____
Security Reference No.(SRN) or Holder Identification No. (HIN): _____
Location of holding statement: _____

Company: _____
Number of shares: _____ Type: _____
Date acquired: _____ Date sold: _____
Security Reference No.(SRN) or Holder Identification No. (HIN): _____
Location of holding statement: _____

Company: _____
Number of shares: _____ Type: _____
Date acquired: _____ Date sold: _____
Security Reference No.(SRN) or Holder Identification No. (HIN): _____
Location of holding statement: _____

Company: _____
Number of shares: _____ Type: _____
Date acquired: _____ Date sold: _____
Security Reference No.(SRN) or Holder Identification No. (HIN): _____
Location of holding statement: _____

Managed Funds

For holdings on the ASX CHESS Share Register, the details of my sponsoring broker are as follows:

Name: _____

Address: _____

Telephone: _____ Email: _____

Contact person: _____

Company: _____

Number of shares or units: _____

Date acquired: _____ Date sold: _____

Account or Investor Number: _____

Location of holding statement: _____

Company: _____

Number of shares or units: _____

Date acquired: _____ Date sold: _____

Account or Investor Number: _____

Location of holding statement: _____

Company: _____

Number of shares or units: _____

Date acquired: _____ Date sold: _____

Account or Investor Number: _____

Location of holding statement: _____

Company: _____

Number of shares or units: _____

Date acquired: _____ Date sold: _____

Account or Investor Number: _____

Location of holding statement: _____

Units in Real Estate Investment Trust Funds

For holdings on the ASX CHESS Share Register, the details of my sponsoring broker are as follows:

Name: _____
Address: _____
Telephone: _____ Email: _____
Contact person: _____

Company: _____
Number of shares or units: _____
Date acquired: _____ Date sold: _____
Account or Investor Number: _____
Location of holding statement: _____

Company: _____
Number of shares or units: _____
Date acquired: _____ Date sold: _____
Account or Investor Number: _____
Location of holding statement: _____

Company: _____
Number of shares or units: _____
Date acquired: _____ Date sold: _____
Account or Investor Number: _____
Location of holding statement: _____

Company: _____
Number of shares or units: _____
Date acquired: _____ Date sold: _____
Account or Investor Number: _____
Location of holding statement: _____

Monetary Investment Details

This section relates to cash management trusts, income securities, etc. For holdings on the ASX CHESS Share Register, the details of my sponsoring broker are as follows:

Name: _____
Address: _____
Telephone: _____ Email: _____
Contact person: _____

Financial institution: _____
Type of investments: _____
Date acquired: _____ Date closed: _____
Account or Investor Number: _____
Location of holding statement: _____
Notes: _____
_____

Financial institution: _____
Type of investments: _____
Date acquired: _____ Date closed: _____
Account or Investor Number: _____
Location of holding statement: _____
Notes: _____
_____

Financial institution: _____
Type of investments: _____
Date acquired: _____ Date closed: _____
Account or Investor Number: _____
Location of holding statement: _____
Notes: _____
_____

Motor Vehicles

For motorised vehicles of all types: cars, motorbikes, airplanes, boats, trucks, tractors, quad bikes and so on.

Type: _____
Registration number: _____
Date acquired: _____ Date disposed of: _____
Location of certificate of registration: _____
Insured by: _____ Policy number: _____
Financed or leased through: _____
Held on behalf of: _____

Type: _____
Registration number: _____
Date acquired: _____ Date disposed of: _____
Location of certificate of registration: _____
Insured by: _____ Policy number: _____
Financed or leased through: _____
Held on behalf of: _____

Type: _____
Registration number: _____
Date acquired: _____ Date disposed of: _____
Location of certificate of registration: _____
Insured by: _____ Policy number: _____
Financed or leased through: _____
Held on behalf of: _____

Type: _____
Registration number: _____
Date acquired: _____ Date disposed of: _____
Location of certificate of registration: _____
Insured by: _____ Policy number: _____
Financed or leased through: _____
Held on behalf of: _____

Type: _____
Registration number: _____
Date acquired: _____ Date disposed of: _____
Location of certificate of registration: _____
Insured by: _____ Policy number: _____
Financed or leased through: _____
Held on behalf of: _____

Type: _____
Registration number: _____
Date acquired: _____ Date disposed of: _____
Location of certificate of registration: _____
Insured by: _____ Policy number: _____
Financed or leased through: _____
Held on behalf of: _____

Type: _____
Registration number: _____
Date acquired: _____ Date disposed of: _____
Location of certificate of registration: _____
Insured by: _____ Policy number: _____
Financed or leased through: _____
Held on behalf of: _____

Private Companies and Businesses

Business Succession Planning is an area that requires the input of both your lawyer and accountant to ensure that the correct mechanisms are in place after considering all of your circumstances.

Consider if you need key-person life insurance or whether a Buy-Sell Agreement is necessary, between you and your business partners, so that the remaining members of the business can purchase the shares of the business when a defined trigger event occurs, such as the death, incapacity or insolvency of one of the shareholders.

Name of business: _____
Registered company/sole proprietor/partnership/trust: _____
ACN/ABN of business: _____
Registered office: _____
Date acquired/commenced: _____
Extent or percentage of my holding: _____
Directors: _____
Other shareholders: _____
_____
_____

Is there a Buy-Sell Agreement: _____
Instructions in the event of my death or incapacity: _____
_____
_____
_____
_____
_____

Name of business: _____
Registered company/sole proprietor/partnership/trust: _____
ACN/ABN of business: _____

Registered office: _____
Date acquired/commenced: _____
Extent or percentage of my holding: _____
Directors: _____
Other shareholders: _____
_____
_____

Is there a Buy-Sell Agreement: _____
Instructions in the event of my death or incapacity: _____
_____
_____
_____
_____
_____

Name of business: _____
Registered company/sole proprietor/partnership/trust: _____
ACN/ABN of business: _____
Registered office: _____
Date acquired/commenced: _____
Extent or percentage of my holding: _____
Directors: _____
Other shareholders: _____
_____
_____

Is there a Buy-Sell Agreement: _____
Instructions in the event of my death or incapacity: _____
_____
_____
_____
_____
_____

Online Business Assets

An online business is open 24/7 taking orders from all over the globe. As with a physical business, you will need a Business Succession Plan. Access details and all relevant information should be available to ensure that your attorney or executor can preserve and deal with them.

Type of asset: _____
What should be done with them: _____
_____

Type of asset: _____
What should be done with them: _____
_____

Dropbox, iCloud, any online data storage: _____
_____
What should be done with them: _____
_____

Dropbox, iCloud, any online data storage: _____
_____
What should be done with them: _____
_____

Digital music and video accounts

It should be noted that any music that you possess on your smartphone or other mp3 player is merely licensed to you. Even if you have an extensive music collection, you cannot transfer or gift this to anyone else, though you can in some instances share. Is there anything to be done with your digital entertainment? __
_____
_____

Other Assets

These can include an interest in a deceased person's estate or property, intellectual property, patents, software, computer applications, copyrights, antiques and artwork, livestock, crops, land rights, water rights, easements, farming equipment, debts payable to you, trade stock, goodwill, life interests in property, property over which you have possession for the purposes of Adverse Possession (where you have had exclusive and uninterrupted possession of land to which you have acted as the owner though you are not the title holder.)

Type of asset: _____
Location of asset: _____
Date acquired: _____ Percentage holding: _____
Co-owners: _____
Other relevant information: _____
_____

Type of asset: _____
Location of asset: _____
Date acquired: _____ Percentage holding: _____
Co-owners: _____
Other relevant information: _____
_____

Type of asset: _____
Location of asset: _____
Date acquired: _____ Percentage holding: _____
Co-owners: _____
Other relevant information: _____
_____

Superannuation and Trusts

My Superannuation

My specific instructions relating to my Super are _____
_____
_____
_____
_____

Date of Binding Death Benefit Nomination: _____
Renewal date of Binding Death Benefit Nomination: _____
I would like my Power of Attorney to withdraw my Super prior to death to save on tax? YES/NO
My attorney is instructed to make a Binding Death Benefit Nomination: YES/NO
My instructions relating to a Binding Death Benefit Nomination are _____
_____
_____

Copies of my instructions to my Power of Attorney are kept _____
_____

My Superannuation fund, including Self-Managed Super Funds (SMSF)

Name of fund: _____ Membership number: _____
Address: _____
Telephone: _____ Email: _____
Nominated beneficiaries: _____
_____

Name of fund: _____ Membership number: _____
Address: _____
Telephone: _____ Email: _____
Nominated beneficiaries: _____
_____

Name of fund: _____ Membership number: _____
Address: _____
Telephone: _____ Email: _____
Nominated beneficiaries: _____
_____

Name of fund: _____ Membership number: _____
Address: _____
Telephone: _____ Email: _____
Nominated beneficiaries: _____
_____

Name of fund: _____ Membership number: _____
Address: _____
Telephone: _____ Email: _____
Nominated beneficiaries: _____
_____

Name of fund: _____ Membership number: _____
Address: _____
Telephone: _____ Email: _____
Nominated beneficiaries: _____
_____

Name of fund: _____ Membership number: _____
Address: _____
Telephone: _____ Email: _____
Nominated beneficiaries: _____
_____

Superannuation Pensions

If you opt to receive a pension from your Super, rather than a lump sum, you should nominate a reversionary pensioner, i.e. the person who will receive your pension once you pass away, such as your partner. It is difficult for another family member to challenge a reversionary pension.

> TIP: Pension can be tax free if the recipient is 60 or older.

There are a limited number of people who can claim a reversionary pension, being the surviving spouse, a minor child (but must be cashed in once they reach 25), or a disabled adult child. The tax-free nature of the pension continues to the reversionary. Your child's guardian will receive the pension payment on their behalf.

Life interest pension from a Self-Managed Super Fund (SMSF)

It is possible for the member of an SMSF to nominate that their spouse has a life interest in the pension with the remainder passing to the member's children on the death of the spouse. Please note that the tax office has yet to make a ruling on this mechanism, therefore you should proceed with caution and only after obtaining up to date advice from your tax accountant.

My Pensions

I am entitled to the following pensions and Centrelink benefits:

Name of pension/benefit: _____
Nature of pension: _____
Commencement: _____
The reversionary pensioner is: _____

Notes: _____
_____

Name of pension/benefit: _____
Nature of pension: _____
Commencement: _____
The reversionary pensioner is: _____
Notes: _____
_____

Name of pension/benefit: _____
Nature of pension: _____
Commencement: _____
The reversionary pensioner is: _____
Notes: _____
_____

Name of pension/benefit: _____
Nature of pension: _____
Commencement: _____
The reversionary pensioner is: _____
Notes: _____
_____

Powers of Attorney and the Withdrawal of Super before Death.

If the fund member has reached retirement age, it is possible for them to withdraw their Super tax-free. If you have a Power of Attorney, they may opt, or you may instruct them, to withdraw the funds, before your death to avoid tax. This principle can also apply if you become terminally ill. Please refer to the section on the withdrawal of Super for further instances where this mechanism can be utilised.

My Trust Interests

I am a beneficiary of the following trusts:

Name of Discretionary Trust: _____
Trustee: _____
Address: _____
Telephone: _____
Contact person: _____ Email: _____
Location of trust deed: _____
Other beneficiaries: _____

Special directions or notes: _____
_____
_____
_____

Name of Unit Trust: _____
Trustee: _____
Address: _____
Contact person: _____ Telephone: _____
Email: _____
My benefit: _____
Location of trust deed: _____
Names and addresses of unitholders
Name: _____
Address: _____
Name: _____
Address: _____
Special directions or notes: _____
_____
_____
_____

I am the trustee of the following trusts:

Name and type of trust: _____

Contact person: _____ Telephone: _____

Email: _____

Location of trust deed: _____

Beneficiaries: _____

_____

Special directions or notes: _____

_____

_____

_____

Name and type of trust: _____

Contact person: _____ Telephone: _____

Email: _____

Location of trust deed: _____

Beneficiaries: _____

_____

Special directions or notes: _____

_____

_____

_____

Executorships

Executor to the estate of: _____
Date of appointment: _____ Distributed estate: _____
Notes: _____
_____
_____
_____

Executor to the estate of: _____
Date of appointment: _____ Distributed estate: _____
Notes: _____
_____
_____

Executor to the estate of: _____
Date of appointment: _____ Distributed estate: _____
Notes: _____
_____
_____
_____

Executor to the estate of: _____
Date of appointment: _____ Distributed estate: _____
Notes: _____
_____
_____
_____

Powers to Appoint

A power to appoint refers to the power granted in a deed of trust to appoint a new trustee.

I have the following powers to appoint a trustee, controller, appointer, or beneficiary under a Will or trust:

Name of trust or estate: _____
Contact details: _____
Specifics of power given: _____
Notes, considerations to be taken or how I have exercised this power: _____
_____
_____
_____

Letter of Wishes to My Trustee

As a Will-maker or trust settlor you can draft a Letter of Wishes to guide to your executors and trustees, and alert them to factors that should be taken into consideration, both in the management of the trust and the needs of the beneficiaries.

This letter is often separate and may be kept private between you and the trustees. It should be clear that the letter is not a testamentary document, such as a new Will or Codicil, or letter of instructions but merely an expression of your wishes. If you wish to make a binding direction, it should be included in your Will or trust deed.

Please refer to www.the-life-manual.com for an example and template of a letter of wishes.

Personal Items

Sentimental Possessions

This section is not intended to override your Will and it is not binding on your executors. If it is your wish that certain items be left to specific individuals, it is best to provide for that in your Will. If you do so you should consider including a clause in your Will relating to ademption, meaning that your executor is only required to give the item specified if you actually own it when you die. Such a clause will usually say something like this:

"Any disposition made in this Will is subject to my retaining an interest in the property to be disposed of."

This means that if you no longer have the item that you have gifted to someone when you die, your executors are not obliged to locate it and obtain it for your beneficiary.

Some items of sentimental value, such as family photos, can cause immense disruption and fighting. It is best to make specific provisions for such items.

You may also consider including a clause in your Will relating to your non-binding direction to your executors to pass on the items as noted here, by stating:

"It is my strong wish that my Executors distribute my chattels in accordance with any list I may leave stored with my Will or amongst my private papers and signed by me, PROVIDED THAT if I fail to leave such a list, or to the extent that any of my chattels are not listed or distributed, they will devolve to the residue of my estate."

It is my general wish that my sentimental and personal items be dealt with as follows: _____
_____
_____

It is my strong, but non-binding wish that my executors give the following items to the individuals named.

Name: _____
Item: _____
Location of item: _____
Reason: _____
_____

Name: _____
Item: _____
Location of item: _____
Reason: _____
_____

Name: _____
Item: _____
Location of item: _____
Reason: _____
_____

Name: _____
Item: _____
Location of item: _____
Reason: _____
_____

Name: _____
Item: _____
Location of item: _____
Reason: _____
_____

Alternatively:

Name	Item	Location of item/why

Signed: _____ Dated: _____

My Personal Possessions

The following is not intended to be a testamentary instruction to my executors. I expect that there will be some of my personal and household items that are of no value (financial, sentimental or otherwise) to my estate or beneficiaries.

These items may be of some value to a charity or other person or entity and I would hope that these items are dealt with as follows:

Items	What could be done with them

Items in my Possession that Do Not Belong to Me

Perhaps you're a regular borrower from the library or DVD shop and wish to make sure that these items are returned. Make a note so that your family will be able to tie up the loose ends more easily.

    Or perhaps you are just holding onto something for someone or you are a secret trustee.

***

The following items may be in my possession, but do not belong to me. Please return them to their rightful owner.

Item: _____
Owners: _____
Contact details: _____

Item: _____
Owners: _____
Contact details: _____

Item: _____
Owners: _____
Contact details: _____

Item: _____
Owners: _____
Contact details: _____

Item: _____
Owners: _____
Contact details: _____

Heirlooms

I have the following heirlooms:

Item: _____
Who it used to belong to: _____
The story behind it: _____
_____
Who should have it (remember this is non-binding, so if you wish to dispose of it on your death, you should make a note of it in your Will): _____
Reason: _____
_____

Item: _____
Who it used to belong to: _____
The story behind it: _____
_____
Who should have it (remember this is non-binding, so if you wish to dispose of it on your death, you should make a note of it in your Will): _____
Reason: _____
_____

Item: _____
Who it used to belong to: _____
The story behind it: _____
_____
Who should have it (remember this is non-binding, so if you wish to dispose of it on your death, you should make a note of it in your Will): _____
Reason: _____
_____

Liabilities

The management of debt and liability can make or break the attainment of a financial goal.

Further, in the administration of your estate, your executor will be obliged to settle all debts before paying any inheritances. If your debts exceed your assets and your estate is insolvent, your executor or administrator will need to dispose of the assets and pay the debts. Secured debts are paid in full including the associated costs of recovery. Any other proceeds will be distributed pro-rata to the remaining unsecured creditors.

If a creditor takes recovery steps it is important to question any recovery costs that are claimed from you. To do this you will need to obtain a break-down of those costs and, if unreasonable, take the matter up either with the Court or with the regulatory body that governs that particular service provider. Some organisations will charge higher fees when there are available funds to cover them.

Maintain a record of all agreements and correspondence relating to the obligation and make a note below of where that information can be found. This will assist your executor or administrator in defending a claim brought against you or your estate.

My Liabilities

Other than my regular accounts, the mortgages on my properties or the motor vehicle financing that I have already specified, I have the following liabilities:

Secured Debts

Indebted to: _____

Contact details: _____

_____

Date of debt: _____ Date debt repaid: _____
Amount of debt: _____
How debt is being repaid: _____
Property on which debt is secured: _____
Documents evidencing debt: _____
Notes: _____
_____
_____

Indebted to: _____
Contact details: _____
_____
Date of debt: _____ Date debt repaid: _____
Amount of debt: _____
How debt is being repaid: _____
Property on which debt is secured: _____
Documents evidencing debt: _____
Notes: _____
_____
_____

Indebted to: _____
Contact details: _____
_____
Date of debt: _____ Date debt repaid: _____
Amount of debt: _____
How debt is being repaid: _____
Property on which debt is secured: _____
Documents evidencing debt: _____
Notes: _____
_____
_____
_____

Unsecured Debts

Indebted to: _____
Contact details: _____
Date of debt: _____ Date debt repaid: _____
Amount of debt: _____
How debt is being repaid: _____
Documents evidencing debt: _____
Notes: _____
_____
_____

Indebted to: _____
Contact details: _____
Date of debt: _____ Date debt repaid: _____
Amount of debt: _____
How debt is being repaid: _____
Documents evidencing debt: _____
Notes: _____
_____
_____

Indebted to: _____
Contact details: _____
Date of debt: _____ Date debt repaid: _____
Amount of debt: _____
How debt is being repaid: _____
Documents evidencing debt: _____
Notes: _____
_____
_____

Guarantees

I am guarantor for the following people or transactions:

Guarantee in favour of: _____
Contact details: _____
_____
On behalf of: _____
Contact details: _____
Date of debt: _____ Date debt repaid: _____
Amount of debt: _____ How debt is being repaid: _____
Documents evidencing guarantee: _____
Notes: _____
_____
_____
_____

Guarantee in favour of: _____
Contact details: _____
_____
On behalf of: _____
Contact details: _____
Date of debt: _____ Date debt repaid: _____
Amount of debt: _____ How debt is being repaid: _____
Documents evidencing guarantee: _____
Notes: _____
_____
_____
_____

Tax

Tax is an inescapable obligation. Indeed, the tax man is sticking his hands so deep into your pockets that you could be forgiven for thinking that he could have at least bought you dinner first! That is why it is important to have a tax adviser who will keep abreast of the changes, as well as the ongoing obligations that you will have, both while living and after you pass away.

The purpose of the section is NOT to provide you with tax advice, as the information provided here is of a general nature only and is no substitute for the advice of a tax accountant or similarly qualified advisor.

For Capital Gains Tax (CGT) purposes, you must keep accurate records of every transaction, prescribed event or relevant factor as it relates to the calculation of your capital gain or loss. If you think you could be liable for CGT, or any other tax obligation, please check with you tax advisor as to what information should be retained. These records could include:

1. The date and price you purchased the asset;
2. The date and price that you sold the asset;
3. Any costs incurred in buying or selling the asset;
4. Improvement and maintenance expenses;
5. Work you performed to maintain or improve the asset.

Information relating to my tax obligations can be found: _____
I received CGT or tax advice on: _____
From: _____
In specific relation to: _____
To deal with my tax affairs as follows: _____
_____
_____
_____

Location of receipts relating to expenses to be offset against CGT: _____
_____

You should obtain the advice in writing and keep a copy with your records.

After your death, your executor may be obliged to lodge a tax return for the current tax year up to the time of your death. Your estate may be entitled to a refund on over-paid taxes.

Your estate becomes a separate tax payer and may be required to lodge its own returns. If your executor is unsure, s/he should contact your tax accountant for clarification. You should have this information available for your executor. If you were liable for outstanding tax, and your executor pays out the proceeds of your estate to your beneficiaries without paying the overdue tax, the executor could become personally liable for your tax.

My Tax File Number is: _____

Copies of tax returns can be found: _____

My sources of income, both passive and active are from: _____
_____
_____
_____

I am a resident for tax purposes in the following countries: _____
_____

I am registered for GST, under: _____
_____

I pay land tax for the following properties: _____
_____
_____

Further notes: _____
_____
_____
_____
_____
_____
_____
_____
_____

4

PLANNING FOR THE ALL EVENTUALITIES

If I Become Incapacitated

The reality is that medical science can keep us alive for longer, but as yet it cannot reverse such things as dementia or brain injuries. According to Dementia Australia,[1] 1 in 10 people over the age of 65 years has dementia, increasing to 3 in 10 for over 85-year-olds. While there are some ways to reduce the risk of dementia, based on the premise of 'use it or lose it', such as tango and ballroom dancing, brain training, reading, exercise and a healthy diet, there is no definitive way to avoid it.

It's not just dementia that can lead to incapacity: strokes, disease and injury due to an accident can also leave someone unable to manage their affairs and such incidents can occur at any age. It is, therefore, better to plan now for the possibility that you may become incapacitated, while you still can, even if it never happens.

There could also be degrees of incapacity and for the most part the person that you are is still in there with some awareness of your situation. You want to be heard. Unfortunately, it is often assumed that an incapacitated person can have no say in any of the decisions made. This is simply not true. While such a person is altered, becoming for example more aggressive, they are still present, needing to be heard and treated with dignity.

---

[1] https://fightdementia.org.au/about-dementia/statistics

Therefore, it is recommended that you take this opportunity to make your wishes known and you could research some of the options that might be available to you.

Please consult www.the-life-manual.com for other books and resources in this series relating to incapacity and Powers of Attorney and how you would like your family to assist you if you find yourself in this situation.

My Powers of Attorney

Make a note of the Powers of Attorney that you have executed.

It is important that you appoint the right person. Therefore, if there is someone who should not be appointed, you could make a note of it here. These pages could be taken into consideration by any Tribunal that may be tasked with reviewing your Power of Attorney, or appointing an administrator or guardian to assist you.

You should remember to revoke a Power of Attorney when circumstances change, such as your attorney becomes bankrupt or incapacitated, you no longer trust them, or perhaps your attorney is your former partner.

It is therefore recommended that you obtain legal advice to determine what is right for you.

***

If I do not have an Enduring Power of Attorney at the time of my incapacity, I would be happy if the following people were appointed to be my decision makers:

Date of this direction: _____ Name of person: _____
Reason: _____
_____

Types of decisions I would be happy for this person to make (i.e. financial, medical or life style and guardianship): _____
_____
_____

Date of this direction: _____ Name of person: _____
Reason: _____
_____
_____

Types of decisions I would be happy for this person to make (i.e. financial, medical or life style and guardianship): _____
_____
_____

Date of this direction: _____ Name of person: _____
Reason: _____
_____
_____

Types of decisions I would be happy for this person to make (i.e. financial, medical or life style and guardianship): _____
_____
_____

I do not want the following people making decisions for my care and finances:

Date of this direction: _____ Name of person: _____
Reason: _____
_____
_____
_____

Date of this direction: _____ Name of person: _____
Reason: _____
_____
_____
_____

Other considerations for my decision makers: _____
_____
_____
_____
_____
_____
_____
_____
_____
_____

Powers of Attorney I have executed

Date: _____ Type of power: _____
Given to: _____
Alternative attorney/agent: _____
Extent of power: _____
Commencement date or event: _____
Enduring? Yes/No: _____ Date revoked or lapsed: _____

Date: _____ Type of power: _____
Given to: _____
Alternative attorney/agent: _____
Extent of power: _____
Commencement date or event: _____
Enduring? Yes/No: _____ Date revoked or lapsed: _____

Date: _____ Type of power: _____
Given to: _____
Alternative attorney/agent: _____
Extent of power: _____
Commencement date or event: _____
Enduring? Yes/No: _____ Date revoked or lapsed: _____

My Living Will or Advanced Care Directive

It is important to execute a Medical Power of Attorney appointing someone who can make medical decisions on your behalf when you are unable to do so. Even if you do have a Medical Power of Attorney, there are some decisions that your appointed attorney cannot make, such as those relating to sterilisation and the termination of a pregnancy.

Please consult www.the-life-manual.com for other books and resources in this series relating to Incapacity and Powers of Attorney, and how you would like your family to assist you during such a time.

Notes: _____
_____
_____
_____
_____
_____
_____
_____
_____
_____
_____
_____
_____
_____
_____
_____
_____
_____
_____
_____

Insurance

When you die or should you become incapacitated, your executor or guardian will need to know if s/he can claim on insurance.

Life Insurance

Life insurance can be obtained either through Super or directly through an insurer. The owner can be the life insured, your business or employer (in respect of key-person insurance) or even your ex-spouse (for the purposes of funding future child support).

Life insurance benefits are paid directly to the beneficiary and do not form part of your estate, unless nominated. This protects the benefit from claims against your estate and ensures the beneficiary will receive the sum insured. When drafting your Will remember that this money will be dealt with in this manner.

If your life insurance benefit is paid out to a child, the proceeds will be placed in a trust and the child taxed on the income at ordinary marginal rates and not penalty rates as would otherwise apply to a child.

Insurer: _____
Address: _____
Telephone: _____
Documents relating to cover are located at: _____
Beneficiary: _____
Receipt or policy number: _____
Notes: _____
_____
_____
_____

Insurer: _____
Address: _____
Telephone: _____
Documents relating to cover are located at: _____
Beneficiary: _____
Receipt or policy number: _____
Notes: _____
_____
_____
_____

Other Forms of Insurance

There are numerous forms of insurance, to cover a number of eventualities, such as:

- Key-person Life Insurance (re Buy-Sell Agreements);
- Disability Insurance;
- Household Insurance;
- Renters Insurance;
- Car Insurance;
- Pet Insurance;
- Health Insurance;
- Business Insurance;
- Professional Indemnity;
- Loss of Earnings.

What would happen if something occurred in one of the above mentioned areas of your life? Would you be greatly affected? Do the benefits of insurance outweigh the costs?

Insurer: _____ Type of insurance: _____
Address: _____
Telephone: _____
Documents relating to cover are located at: _____
Beneficiary: _____
Receipt or policy number: _____
Notes: _____
_____

Insurer: _____ Type of insurance: _____
Address: _____
Telephone: _____
Documents relating to cover are located at: _____
Beneficiary: _____
Receipt or policy number: _____
Notes: _____
_____

Insurer: _____ Type of insurance: _____
Address: _____
Telephone: _____
Documents relating to cover are located at: _____
Beneficiary: _____
Receipt or policy number: _____
Notes: _____
_____

Insurer: _____ Type of insurance: _____
Address: _____
Telephone: _____
Documents relating to cover are located at: _____
Beneficiary: _____
Receipt or policy number: _____
Notes: _____

Estate Planning and Asset Protection Instruments

The purpose of this book is to give you an overview of your entire financial position and goals. There are some estate planning and asset protection mechanisms which may be of interest to you. What follows is a brief overview of some of the options available to you, which you may wish to explore further with your professional advisors.

Trusts

A trust is a mechanism by which the owner of the property does not hold it for themselves, but for the benefit of others. The owner, or trustee, will manage the assets while acting in the best interests of the beneficiaries and not in their own interests.

Advantages of a trust

- **Protection** - The trust assets are protected from a spendthrift beneficiary, or in the event of bankruptcy, from the beneficiaries' creditors.
- **Keeping it in the family** - The trust could specify that the creator's children only have access to trust income (and not that child's spouse) with the ultimate beneficiaries being the grandchildren, keeping the money in the family.
- **Loans to beneficiaries** - If the trust makes a loan to a beneficiary, for example to buy a home, that could stand as an obligation payable by that person.
    - The trust could offer favourable terms.
    - This resource is somewhat protected in the event of a relationship breakdown or insolvency, so that only the intended beneficiary will ultimately benefit.
    - The trust could place a mortgage on the property to secure that loan. To remain a valid obligation, some form of repayment, even if nominal, must be made, failing which, after six years, the loan will lapse.

Disadvantages of a trust

- In a family law scenario, a beneficiary's interest under a trust must be disclosed as it is a potential financial resource in the event of a relationship breakdown property claim, particularly where a degree of control exists over the trust assets by this person, such as being a trustee or appointor.
    - The appointment of an independent trustee may alleviate this issue. If the beneficiary is an appointor they will be deemed to have control over the trust, because they can appoint a new trustee.
    - If there are a number of beneficiaries, some of whom also have control over the trust, the Court in family law proceedings may be less likely to consider that a beneficiary has adequate control over the trust assets, and so may be disregard the trust as a financial resource of that beneficiary.
- Carefully consider if it is appropriate that the family home is owned by a trust:
    - Capital Gains Tax will apply, as you will not be able to claim the Principal Place of Residence exemption.
    - Annual land tax may also be payable on the same basis, depending on the State in which the property is situated.

Implied Trusts

These are trusts that may not have been specifically declared but implied by operation of law.

There are two types of Implied Trusts:
1. Constructive Trusts;
2. Resulting Trusts.

Constructive Trusts

- This is a trust constructed in law. A title holder is deemed to hold the property, in whole or in part, for the benefit of someone else.
- A common example of this is where one spouse is the title holder and the other makes financial or non-financial contributions to the property.
- A trust will be constructed in favour of the non-title holder, for the sake of equity and fairness, because of those contributions.
- It is possible to lodge a caveat over the property on the basis of a Constructive Trust to protect your interests.

Resulting Trusts

- A Resulting Trust is said to arise when property is transferred to someone else for the purpose of creating a trust, but for some reason that trust fails, for example where there are no beneficiaries. A trust cannot exist where there are no beneficiaries.
- Therefore, a trust is implied in favour of the person who transferred the property to the person who was supposed to be the trustee of the failed trust.

Express Trusts

There are various types of Express Trusts, i.e. trusts that are formed intentionally, and in writing, whether testamentary or during your life time by trust deed.

What follows on the next page is a brief overview of the common express trusts available.

Discretionary Trusts
- The trustee has the discretion to make a distribution to any of the beneficiaries within the defined class of beneficiaries.

Life Interest Trusts
- The primary beneficiary has the right to the full use of a particular property for so long as they live, thereafter the property passes to the nominated remainder beneficiaries.

Accommodation Fund Trusts
- To pay for the accommodation needs of the beneficiary thereafter the funds pass to remainder beneficiaries.

Right of Occupation Trusts
- A personal right with no commercial value, cannot be transferred. Once the primary beneficiary ceases occupation, for whatever reason, the trust terminates. No CGT payable by primary beneficiary.

Protective Trusts
- **Special Disability Trusts** - For the protection of a disabled person. Subject to Centrelink rules.
- **Childrens' Trusts** - until child reaches specified age.

Educational Trusts
- Trust established to maintain child during their education.

Capital Reserved Trusts
- Primary beneficiary only entitled to trust income, remainder beneficiry receives capital on death of primary beneficiary.

Testamentary Trust
- Any of the Express Trusts established through a Will, usually discretionary.
- Can be a Beneficiary Controlled Testamentary Trust.

Estate Proceeds Trust
- Established by a beneficiary under a Will and not in the Will itself.

Discretionary Trusts

As with any trust, a Discretionary Trust can be established during your lifetime or through your Will. Discretionary Trusts grant the trustee a discretion as to whom they shall distribute either the income or the capital from the trust, from a defined group of beneficiaries.

Advantage of a Discretionary Trust

- **Income splitting** - The income from the trust can be distributed to beneficiaries in the most tax efficient manner. Lower threshold tax payers may receive more, so that less tax overall is paid. Note however that a child will be taxed at penalty rates if the funds are not sourced through a deceased estate (e.g. a lifetime family trust) or other excepted circumstances.
    - Though if a minor is in full time employment, is incapacitated or a double orphan, they will be taxed at the ordinary rate.
- **Asset protection** - To protect the assets from the beneficiaries' creditors or the beneficiary themselves.
- **Vulnerable beneficiaries** - To protect the assets where a beneficiary may be unable to manage their money themselves due to their lack of capacity.
- **Flexibility** - This allows the trust to distribute in a tax efficient or needs based manner.
- **Different classes of income** - A trust may hold different assets that earn an income, for example rental income and dividends.
    - The trustee can choose how to distribute the income. A trustee could opt to distribute dividends income with the franking credits (i.e. tax credits in respect of tax already paid by the company that issued the dividends) to a beneficiary who has income beyond the tax free threshold, to offset their tax liability.
    - The trustee may distribute the rental or other income to a beneficiary who is yet to reach the tax threshold to create a more efficient tax scenario for the beneficiaries. Of course to do so, the trustee must be made aware of these advantages.

Disadvantages of a Discretionary Trust

- **Trustee bias or incompetence** - The trustee may bias certain beneficiaries, though the trustee is required to exercise their discretion in good faith.
- **Family law or tax liability** - The assets could be deemed a financial resource of a beneficiary for family law property claims or tax purposes.

> TIP: Provide the trustee with a Letter of Wishes, i.e. a non-binding framework around which the trust is to be managed and which serves as a guide to the exercise of discretion.

A Letter of Wishes expresses who you would prefer to receive a benefit, as well as contingent beneficiaries and the age upon which funds are to vest in younger beneficiaries, such as at the age of 21 or 25. It is important to update your Letter of Wishes from time to time, particularly as circumstances change.

Life Interests

A Life Interest in property is a type of trust, usually created in a Will, in which a person is entitled to the use and enjoyment of a particular piece of property for the remainder of their life, including all income generated from the property or trust. The property is held in trust for the ultimate beneficiary (a capital beneficiary) who will then have full rights in the property after the life tenant (an income beneficiary) dies. One could provide for a Life Interest in any asset.

> CONSIDER: Income derived from a Life Interest is taxable.

Advantages of Life Tenancies:

- **Multi-generational beneficiaries -** A Life Interest trust is commonly used where the Will-maker wants their spouse or partner to have the use of the family home until they die and thereafter the Will-maker's children inherit the property. This is of particular significance in second marriages where the Will-maker wants his or her children to ultimately inherit the property, rather than their partner/spouse's children, as could otherwise occur if the property were left in full to the spouse.
- **Family provision obligations -** Where you have a duty to provide for someone, such as a spouse, you can do so with the Life Interest, while ensuring the property ultimately passes to someone of your choosing.
- **Registrable -** As this is a property right, the life tenant can register their interest on title, which can prevent the property being dealt with in opposition with their interests, which is particularly useful for vulnerable persons.

Disadvantages of a Life Interest

- **Complex -** Life Interests are best drafted by a legal practitioner. There are a number of considerations that should be taken into account:
    - Who is to pay for the rates and maintenance of the property? Who is to insure the property?
    - What should happen if the life tenant can no longer reside at the property and needs to be placed in care? Should the property then be sold to pay the life tenant's nursing home bond. This would undermine the value of this mechanism.
    - Therefore, it is imperative to specify how such a trust should terminate, or whether a mortgage could be placed over the property for the purposes of a nursing home bond.
- **Changes in circumstance -** This form of trust can exist for a number of years and the circumstances of all beneficiaries could alter considerably during this time to an extent that may not be anticipated.

- **Not necessarily a guard against claims** - Current legislation states that a domestic partner or dependent can claim against your estate if you fail to make adequate provision for him/her in your Will. A Life Interest will not necessarily defeat such a claim, and if the surviving partner were to require funds for a nursing home bond for example, that is when a claim would likely be made.
- **Tax on early surrender** - If the trust is surrendered early, there could be Capital Gains Tax consequences for the life tenant, either based on the consideration that the life tenant receives, or if the surrender is for nil consideration, the Tax Office will then base the capital gain or loss on the market value of the Life Interest that is surrendered. Any CGT consequences are usually disregarded if the life tenant remains with the interest intact until the time of his/her death. This could also change at any time.
- **Conflicting interests of the beneficiaries** - Your trustee will need to balance the conflicting interests of the two classes of beneficiaries: the income beneficiary seeking investment with a high income return and the remainder beneficiaries seeking capital growth, particularly if they are waiting a number of years to receive the property.

> The CGT Principal Place of Residence exemption also applies to a domestic partner with a life interest, but not for a substitute residence.

Accommodation Fund Trust

This is a portable Life Interest not fixed to a particular piece of property that ensures the accommodation needs of the surviving domestic partner (or any other specified person) are met, in particular to account for his/her changing circumstances.

The Will-maker can provide that the domestic partner (usually) has a right to live in the existing family home during his or her lifetime, but that substitute accommodation be provided from the estate. Once the surviving spouse dies, the Will specifies to whom the remaining trust assets will go.

> TAKE NOTE: CGT can be payable once the substituted residence is sold. You should check with your tax adviser.

Right of Occupation and Use and Enjoyment Trusts

Similar to a Life Interest, the Will-maker grants someone the right to occupy property. This is a lesser right than a Life Interest for as soon as the beneficiary chooses to no longer occupy the property, the right lapses and the property passes to the ultimate beneficiary.

The Right of Occupation could also be framed as a Use and Enjoyment Trust, and such terminology is more apt where the asset in question is not related to land, where the beneficiary can use the asset and take the income produced from that asset.

> TAKE NOTE: The Court can vary a Will containing a Right of Occupation to make a lump sum payment to a domestic partner to fund a Refundable Accommodation Deposit, where the property is no longer suitable to the needs of the occupier.

Advantages to the Right of Occupation Trust

- **Tax savings** - When granted with respect to the Principal Place of Residence of the deceased, the CGT Principal Place of Residence Exemption applies, and CGT is not payable.
- **No presumption of life long obligation** - The right to occupy does not imply that the Will-maker intended to provide that beneficiary with a residence for life. This addresses the issues relating to a Life Interest and the possible sale of the asset to provide for this person moving into aged care.

Disadvantages of Right of Occupation Trust

- **Conflict in beneficiaries' interests -** Again you will need to consider which party is to be responsible for the various outgoings and maintenance in relation to the property.
    - It is possible to have the occupier pay the general maintenance and ongoing costs.
    - The remainder beneficiaries could be made responsible for any improvements or capital expenditure where the benefits of such expenditure add to the value of the property. It is not in the occupier's interest to maintain the property for the benefit of someone else.
    - You should clarify this issue in your Will or trust deed.
- **Family disputes -** If there is conflict between the occupying beneficiary and the ultimate beneficiary, a problem particularly common in step families, regarding who will be responsible for the various costs and maintenance of the property, your trustee will be burdened with continual disputes and may choose to resign if the task becomes too onerous.

> TIP: The terminating events for the Right of Occupation, should be specified, such as no longer residing in the property, ceasing to reside in the property for a certain period of time, the beneficiary's death, on a specified date or the beneficiary's remarriage.

Special Needs, Special Disability or Protective Trusts

These are usually a form of Testamentary Trust. However, these trusts can be established during a person's lifetime. A trust of this nature is established to protect the needs of those who are unable to manage their affairs, for whatever reason, such as an intellectual disability, substance abuse, lack of capacity or even for someone easily influenced.

The trust is used to take care of the needs of the individual, such as accommodation, food, education and ordinary living expenses.

> TIP: check with Centrelink before establishing such a trust to ensure that you do not contravene the Centrelink rules and possibly deprive the beneficiary of some form of Centrelink benefit.

Advantages of Special Needs Trust

- **Protection** - Ensures a vulnerable family member is taken care of, provided there are sufficient funds.
- **Tax management** - If you have a child who suffers from a severe disability, you should consult with a lawyer to establish a Special Disability Trust, and to discuss the tax savings and Centrelink implications, if established during your lifetime. This protective trust is subject to means testing. However, the home is not factored into the calculation up to a certain value, the maximum value of which is adjusted each year.

Disadvantages of Special Needs Trust

- **A long term commitment**
  - The trustee should be one who will be able to manage the trust for the rest of the beneficiary's life, such as a sibling of the beneficiary or a trustee company.
  - It is a long term commitment and the appropriate person should be appointed.
  - You should specify an alternative trustee in case your first choice is unable to take on the appointment.
- **Unexpected circumstances**
  - The trustee's powers should be defined, such as how to invest, what expenses are to be catered for, and how to deal with specific assets.

- Rigidity should be avoided so that the trustee does not need to go to Court to seek authority to deal with an asset in a specific manner, the costs of which will be paid from the trust.
- Allow some flexibility so that the trustee can invest in a tax efficient manner even as tax laws change.

> REMEMBER: You should also nominate who is to receive the residue of the trust when the beneficiary dies.

Children's Trusts

A subcategory of Protective Trusts are children's or minors' trusts. It is common to provide that children will only receive their inheritance when they reach a certain age. Without really thinking about it, most Will-makers include this sort of trust in their Will whenever they specify the age their child should inherit or how their children's share should be managed until they reach adulthood.

The trustee does not need to be the child's guardian, and it is preferable that the two functions are separated to ensure accountability. The trustee will communicate with the guardian and consider the reasonableness of various expenses to be paid from the trust and whether such expenses are authorised.

The trustee will be accountable to the child when he/she reaches adulthood and can apply to Court for an order for compensation if there has been any mismanagement. Likewise, the guardian can commence proceedings against the trustee, usually through the appointment of a litigation guardian who will act on the child's behalf, for the appointment of a new trustee or other remedy.

Education Trusts

Just as you may establish a trust whilst alive to secure the educational needs of your children, or even grandchildren, you can also do so in your Will. This type of trust ensures the availability of funds for further education. You should specify what level of education is provided to ensure that your beneficiaries aren't tempted to become permanent students.

Advantages of Education Trusts

- **Fairness** - The Education Trust ensures that all your children are treated fairly as regards their educational expenses and that the younger children do not have to self-fund their education, particularly tertiary education. This applies especially if you may have paid for the elder children's tuition already and want each of your children to be treated equally.
- **Contained class of beneficiaries** - The balance of funds remaining after the educational purpose has been satisfied is then distributed to the specified remaining beneficiaries.
- **Ease of establishment** - This kind of trust can be established during your lifetime, but it is most often established through a Will.

> TIP: Be sure to define to what level of education your child can be entitled to funds from the trust and the nature of the expenses covered. Should it include accommodation, books, extra tuition and so forth? The underlying principal is equal opportunity for each child.

Capital Reserve Trusts

This is similar to a Life Interest. However, this type of trust is often established by you in your lifetime. The Principal Lifetime Beneficiary, for example yourself or your partner, is entitled to the income from the trust, and may have a right of occupation in any property contained within the trust. There can also be Discretionary Income Beneficiaries, such as your children who do not have an automatic right to income (unlike the Principal Lifetime Beneficiary) but the trustee can decide to give them some of the trust income, which offers some flexibility.

After the Lifetime Beneficiary dies, the Capital Beneficiaries become entitled to the remaining capital in the trust.

Advantages of Capital Reserve Trusts

- **Multi-generational** - The remainder, or capital, beneficiaries will receive the capital when the Lifetime Beneficiary dies.
- **Protective** - This offers protection against creditors (though please refer to the section regarding insolvency) and in family law claims against the Lifetime Beneficiary who has no access to the capital, particularly when the trust established prior to entering into the relationship or with the consent of the domestic partner.

Testamentary Trusts

A Testamentary Trust is the same as any other, except it is established in a Will, rather than operating during the lifetime of the person who establishes the trust.

> TIP: Usually no stamp duty nor CGT is payable when transferring the assets from your deceased estate into a Testamentary Trust, though the estate itself may be liable for CGT. Check with your tax adviser.

- The trust is often discretionary in nature, allowing the trustee to decide which of the beneficiaries named in your Will are to receive funds from the trust. This allows the trustee to take into account the changing needs of beneficiaries.
- The trust comes into effect at the moment of the Will-maker's death, though technically only upon the executor proving the Will in Probate. It can easily be amended prior to death.
    - But if the Will cannot be proved (i.e. accepted as a genuine Will by the Court in a probate application), then the trust does not come into effect. The executor will then be required to prove an older

Will, or your estate will be administered through intestacy if there is no other Will (i.e. the money will go straight to your closest relatives).
- Under intestacy the only trust that can be established is a Children's or Minor's Trust, as a child cannot inherit until they reach the age of 18.

Advantages of a Testamentary Trust

- **The advantages are specific to the sub-type of trust established** - As most Testamentary Trusts are discretionary, please refer to the advantages of Discretionery Trusts, or such other form of trust that you may be considering.
- **Capital Gains advantages** - While the legislation is unclear, the general practice has been that the ATO will disregard any capital gain or loss when an asset passes from a Testamentary Trust to the ultimate beneficiary. This practice could change at any time.
- **Family law advantages** - In the context of family law claims, the general view, though such a view has not been confirmed by the Court, is that a Discretionary Testamentary Trust is a good strategy to protect a beneficiary's inheritance from a family law claim in the event of divorce or *de facto* relationship breakdown.
    - This is because neither party to the relationship has contributed to the trust and the Court is reluctant to undo the Will-maker's intention of benefiting certain people, while excluding the beneficiary's ex-partner.
    - Generally then trust property may not be considered as property belonging to either party to the relationship, though it may be a resource that is available to them, and therefore the trust beneficiary may not be seen to be in need of as great a share of the marital assets when the couple splits up. Unfortunately there really is no other way to protect an inheritance from a family law claim.
- **Tax savings** - Income earned on trust assets will be taxed in the hands of minors at normal adult rates, because they are sourced through a

deceased estate, with the same tax free threshold as adults, and not the penalty rate that ordinarily applies to children under the age of 18 years.

Disadvantages of a Testamentary Trust

- **Administrative costs** - As with any trust there are administrative expenses such as the cost of advisors and other professionals. It is prudent for the trustee to obtain advice from financial planners or tax consultants as to investment strategy or tax efficiency. The trust may also be required to lodge tax returns.
- **Fixed asset base** - Funds cannot be added to a Testamentary Trust from other sources, although the trustee can borrow funds in an ordinary commercial transaction for the benefit of the trust.

Beneficiary Controlled Testamentary Trust

A Testamentary Trust where control of the trust assets, is at a nominated date or event, released to the primary beneficiary but still under the umbrella of the trust.

Advantages of Beneficiary Controlled Testamentary Trust

- **Staggering** - The release of assets can be all at once, or staggered.
- **Self-interest** - The beneficiary could the trustee.
- **Tax** - No CGT is payable on transfer from the estate to the trust, whereas a trust established during the life of the settlor could have CGT consequences.

Estate Proceeds Trust

You can suggest, though it is not binding, that a beneficiary under your Will establishes an Estate Proceeds Trust from their inheritance, that would benefit their children. If you want a binding trust or direction, it must be included in your Will.

Alteratively any beneficiary under a Will can of their own accord establish an Estate Proceeds Trusts within 3 years of the Will-maker's death.

Advantages of Estate Proceeds Trust:

- **Tax savings** - Ordinary marginal rates would apply to children's income (rather than penalty rates) and the income could be used for child related expenses.
- **Delay capital payment** - It could also determine at which age the child receives their payout from the trust once the trust terminates.
- **Multi-generational** - The purpose of such a trust is to protect the interests of the second generation who receive the trust capital. The first generation of beneficiaries are only usually entitled to the trust income, or there can be a deferment of payment of capital to the primary beneficiary.
- **Family law advantage** – This trust can be useful in family law proceedings where there may be claims brought against a first generation beneficiary, who is only entitled to the income from the trust and therefore the trust assets are protected.

Disadvantages of Estate Proceeds Trust

- **Limited** - Such a trust can only be established if the child (being a second generation beneficiary) could have inherited from your estate had you died without a Will, and only to the extent of that benefit received from your estate.
- **Non-mandatory** - As the name suggests this trust is established by the beneficiary of an estate, and not the Will-maker.

- **Time limits** - This trust must be established within three years of the Will-maker's death, and often by the surviving spouse.

Superannuation

Superannuation is the compulsory investment of a portion of your earnings to fund your future retirement. For many people, after the family home, superannuation is the most significant asset.

If you have more than one superannuation account, you may wish to consolidate them to minimise expense.

Withdrawal of Super Funds

Each fund has their particular rules regarding access to Super, you should check with your fund. People usually access their Super in one of the following ways:

Retirement
- Must have reached Preservation Age (between 55 and 60 Years depending on your date of birth).
- Must provide proof of retirement

Reach the age of 65

Transition to Retirement
- You must have reached Preservation Age
- Cannot later opt for a lump sum payout
- You can receive up to 10% of the value of your fund each year as a pension

There are however other means within which to access your Super earlier than is the usual course of events.

> TIP: Consider withdrawing your super as a lump sum payment once you are eligible to do so and then reinvesting it in a separate non-concessional super account in the same fund. Therefore, Death Benefits Tax will not be payable. Check with your Fund and financial planner.

The table on the following page summarises the various methods by which one can access their Super prior to retirement.

Financial Hardship

- Each fund will have its own conditions.
- Can access only some of your Super, as needed.

Terminal Illness

- When you have less than 12 months to live.
- Requires the certificate of two medical practitioners.
- Access to your full fund.

Compassionate Grounds

- For example for funeral or medical expenses, or to prevent the foreclosure on your mortgage.
- Access to amount as per your specific needs.

Fund Member since before 1 July 1999

- You would only have access to your restricted non-preserved balance.
- You must have left your employment.

Permanent Incapacity

- Must be unable to work again.

Temporary Residents

- When leaving Australia permanently.

Persons Eligible to receive your Superannuation Death Benefit

When you die, and have funds in Super, your fund can't give the money to just anyone, even if you nominate them. Eligibility requirements are stipulated by legislation and the trust deed which governs each particular fund. On your death, your death benefits can only be paid to your estate or dependants, failing which it can be paid to anyone the trustees of the fund nominate.

Consider including a term in the trust deed that a child under 25 years is obliged to receive a pension, rather than a lump sum payment to ensure they do not squander it.

Binding Death Benefit Nominations.

Death benefits paid out of Super do not form part of the estate of the deceased person. A Binding Death Benefit Nomination (BDBN) is therefore an important tool to ensure the funds are paid to your desired beneficiary, this usually protects it from claims brought against your estate by creditors or family provision claims, except in New South Wales where the Court may consider your Super as part of your notional estate.

There are formalities to making a BDBN which the fund will specify and usually lasts only 3 years. If the nomination is not valid for any reason, such as one of the beneficiaries has died, the entire nomination usually fails.

> POINT OF CONSIDERATION: Does your Super allow for non-lapsing BDBN? Or only nominations lasting 3 years? Would you remember to change it if your circumstances changed?

Invalid BDBN

It is prudent to make provision in your Will should, for any reason the Binding Death Benefit Nomination fail. For example, the nomination of a step-child is valid only if the deceased is still in a relationship with the child's parent, at the time of death. Further, if the beneficiary is no longer a dependant or in a co-dependent relationship at the time of death, the whole nomination will fail, even the otherwise valid portion. Most Supers do not allow you to specify a contingency plan, in other words it's non-cascading.

Nomination of a Minor

If the nominated beneficiary is a minor, the trustee for the superannuation will establish a separate trust for that child until they reach the age of 18 years. They can appoint the child's surviving parent as trustee. This form of trust will also be established in the absence of a binding nomination. The minor will be taxed at ordinary marginal rates, rather than penalty child rates.

If you are receiving a superannuation payout, you can request that the Super fund establishes a trust for the benefit of your children, for a lower tax liability to the family with the tax free threshold applying, which trust would then make payment to you for child related expenses.

> CONSIDER: Do you want to grant your Financial Power of Attorney the authority to confirm a Binding Death Benefit Nomination when it is reviewed every three years? Or make a BDBN on your behalf? Should they be able to withdraw from your Super and possibly bypass the BDBN? Specify what you want.

Tax on Death Benefits

The taxation of death benefit receipts depends on a number of factors, such as whether the fund itself is taxed or untaxed and whether the beneficiary is a dependent for tax purposes (which has a different definition to a dependent for the purposes of eligibility to receive death benefits). Generally, an actual dependent will not be taxed on death benefits. However, a financially independent adult child who is classified as a dependent for the purposes of eligibility, is not a dependent for tax purposes. Such child will pay tax on benefits received and at differing rates depending on whether the component of the fund is tax free or taxable.

Many of these issues can be avoided if you withdraw your funds after you can gain access, though consideration should be given to whether you would lose concessional tax benefits on your superannuation.

Superannuation Death Benefits Testamentary Trust

You can nominate your Estate to receive your death benefits. Your Will then establishes a Testamentary Trust into which these funds are held. The advantage of such a Trust is that it may contain discretionary beneficiaries. It could be structured in such a way that only those who would receive a tax free benefit, will receive the funds. This is particularly relevant where your children may be dependents when drafting your Will (and therefore a tax free beneficiary) but not at the time of your death. The trust will distribute in the most tax efficient manner.

The beneficiaries of such a trust should only be a surviving spouse or domestic partner, dependent children, inter-dependents and your financial dependents. Tax will be payable if a beneficiary is outside this class of persons. A minor beneficiary will only be taxed at the ordinary rate, and not the penalty rate on any income earned by the trust.

Superannuation Complaints Tribunal (SCT)

If you or a potential beneficiary to your death benefits, are aggrieved by a decision of the trustee of a public superannuation fund, you should firstly request that the trustee reviews their decision. If after review you are still of the opinion that the trustee erred in their decision, you can lodge a complaint with the SCT. There are time constraints, so you should not delay in seeking a review or lodging your complaint.

You should also bear in mind, when putting estate planning measures into effect that this avenue is in existence and you may wish to provide for an equalisation clause in your Will, should the trustee pay out other than how you planned.

Caveats

Where you have an interest in property registered in the name of someone else, for example through a Constructive Trust, you may register a caveat to protect that interest. Constructive Trusts may arise, for example, where you have contributed to the purchase of the property.

A caveat prevents any further dealings on the title of the property, therefore no mortgages or transfers can be registered while your caveat is in place.

Mortgages

If you loan someone money to purchase property, you can register a mortgage over that property, or any of their properties, in the same manner in which a bank does. You do of course need the title holder's consent, which is usually included in the terms and conditions of the loan. This protects your money, but it is vital that you register your mortgage on title straight away, as it is the order of registration on title that carries priority if there are multiple claimants against the property.

Equitable Mortgages

An equitable mortgage is simply one that is not registered on title as such, but that the law provides protection and recognition to secure the interest of the lender.

It is possible, through a carefully documented instrument, to raise an equitable mortgage against your own property in the name of a trust, for example the family home over which the Capital Gains Tax exemption applies, and lodge a caveat to register the trust's interest. Any claim against your property will only be satisfied after the equitable mortgage has been paid due to the registration of the earlier caveat on title.

You may, for example, grant an interest free loan to your child to purchase a house. You may lodge a caveat to protect that interest, being an equitable mortgage. If your child faces family law proceeding your loan will be reflected as a liability, and his or her family home may not be sold without your loan being repaid. You should remember that notional repayments of the loan must be made, failing which after six years the loan lapses. This is a good way to provide for your child and protect that money from claims in family law proceedings or creditors' claims. You should remember to specify in your Will whether this loan should be repaid (or offset) or forgiven.

Bear in mind though that your creditors could enforce payment on this loan as it is an asset to you.

Change in Title

If you are at risk of having your property claimed by creditors, or are engaged in a risky venture, to protect your property you can register it in the name of your spouse.

Advantages of a Change in Title

- **Family law adjustments** - Should you split from your spouse the property will be dealt with according to family law rules where it is usually irrelevant in whose name the property is registered when deciding how to split the joint property.
- **Stamp duty savings** - Stamp duty is not payable in respect of transfer of property between spouses or domestic partners.

- **Tax savings** - There is also no CGT payable on the transfer of the family home, but beware of changing the title of investment properties.
- **Tax management** - For investment properties, where your marginal tax rate is very low, or you have a capital loss on the disposal of another asset, you could offset the Capital Gains Tax that could be payable on the transfer of the property into your partner's name, therefore the timing of the transfer is important. However, you should ensure that no CGT liability accrues due to the transfer.

Disadvantages of Change in Title

- **Claims against spouse** - Your spouse could become insolvent, or have a claim brought against them which threatens the property, but you could lodge a claim based on a Constructive Trust in the property. Likewise, you could also lodge a caveat on the basis of this Constructive Trust, which would give priority to your claim, but care should be taken.
- **Legal uncertainty** - Before doing this though, you should ascertain how the Court in your State are interpreting such transactions to ensure that you get the intended results. It is usually advisable not to over complicate matters. Therefore, it is recommended that you speak to a lawyer, rather than a conveyancer, to register the appropriate transactions.

Buy-Sell Agreements

A Buy-Sell Agreement is one in which business partners agree to purchase the interest in the business of one or more of the other partners on the happening of a certain predefined event. Commonly, the agreement becomes operable in the event of the death, divorce, insolvency, retirement or incapacity of the selling partner.

This is an important tool to ensure that your business is not adversely affected by the personal circumstances of your business partners.

The formula to calculate the purchase price is defined in the agreement and may also include life insurance to ensure payment of the selling price. Please check with your financial or tax adviser to optimise your tax situation and whether there are any possible tax savings.

Without such an agreement in place, protracted disputes can damage the operation of the business and devalue your equity.

Binding Financial Agreements

A Binding Financial Agreement, or BFA, is an agreement entered into between a domestic couple, either married or *de facto*. The agreement stipulates what happens to the parties' assets in the event of a relationship split. There are certain formalities and such an agreement can only be executed through the assistance of a lawyer for each party. Informal agreements, or those that do not meet the legislative requirements are not enforceable in family law proceedings.

Advantages of Binding Financial Agreements

- **A release of your estate** - A BFA should include a release from any claim against your estate or Will.
- **Certainty** - A BFA is an important asset protection mechanism as you can only effectively plan your estate when you know what assets you have to work with.
- **Protection** - If you and your partner split and you became terminally ill, it would be in your former partner's financial interests to bring family law proceedings against you rather than respectfully allowing you to live out the remainder of your days in peace and then make a claim against your estate. Therefore, a BFA can provide some certainty.
    - The reason for this is that family law proceedings will take into account your superannuation fund and your interest in any trust as a financial resource to you, which are not included in your estate.
    - Further, in family law proceedings the Court looks at each of your future financial needs and sadly, as you are about to die, your future financial needs are rather limited. Your former partner could get a fairly substantial slice of the pie.

o Not so if a partner lets you live out your days in peace and claims against your estate. Your ex would have to compete with the needs of the other beneficiaries, and your Super would bypass your estate completely. And the Court would not even look into your other financial resources, such as any trusts to which you were a beneficiary.

Disadvantages of Binding Financial Agreements

- **Overriding by the Court** - In some cases though (particularly in New South Wales) the Court can overrule this Release of a claim against you by your partner on the basis that it is unfair.
  o To create certainty, you may seek the Court's approval of the Release from the outset, thereby creating stability in your estate planning.

Interest Free Loans

If you or your child does not have a BFA and you wanted to offer or receive some financial assistance, you could do so in the form of an interest free loan rather than a gift. This loan would be reclaimable, if so desired, but more importantly it would be reflected as a liability in the borrower's hands which would need to repaid. It would also be reflected in family law proceedings as such, thus reducing the borrower's net worth.

Advantages of Interest Free Loans

- **Protection** - Such a loan protects monies that you would otherwise gift to someone, in insolvency and family law proceedings.
- **Registrable** - This loan could be registered as a mortgage against the borrower's property.
- **Priority** – Alternatively, you could enter into an informal equitable loan, and lodge a caveat on their property to give you first right of recovery in the event of their insolvency or family law proceedings.

Disadvantages of Interest Free Loans

- **Repayments are required** - An important point to remember however is that to keep the loan 'alive' the borrower must make nominal repayments. If no repayments are made on the loan for a period of six years, it becomes irrecoverable and therefore of no use.
- **Further action** - If you make use of such an instrument, which should be in writing, you must decide whether it should be written off in your Will or repaid.
- **Availability to creditors** – The loan is not protected from the lender's creditors or family law claimants. Therefore, a degree of assessment of risk is required of both parties.

Insolvency

Some people may be tempted to transfer their assets to their spouse in order to defeat their creditors' claims. While this does offer a degree of protection, as mentioned earlier, you should be aware that if you or your estate are declared insolvent, your creditors can bring bankruptcy proceedings. A trustee in bankruptcy is empowered to review and reverse certain transfers of assets prior to bankruptcy.

From the point of view of a deceased estate, life insurance payouts and binding superannuation death benefit payments offer protection in insolvency, as do retirement savings accounts, because such funds bypass your estate and go directly to your beneficiaries.

5

WHEN I PASS AWAY

Organ Donation

"All death reminds us that nothing is promised, only that life was worth it."
Shannon L. Alder, 300 Questions to Ask Your Parents Before It's Too Late

Organ donation is a second chance at life for many. It is the ultimate gift you can give. According to Donate Life Australia,[2] there are 1,600 Australians on the donor waiting list at any one time. However, in 2014, there were only 117 Victorian organ donors.

A single donor can help many by donating organs such as their kidneys, liver, heart, lungs, cornea and so on. You can make a difference to many, though it is not an easy decision and considerations of your family's views are important.

Everyone has a different view on the issue of organ donation. You should consult the website http://www.donatelife.gov.au/ to obtain more information on this issue and the legal requirements to leave directions about organ and tissue donation. You should register your decision to become an organ donor as this will ensure that if you have viable organs the medical professionals can act quickly.

---

[2] http://www.donatelife.gov.au/victorians-encouraged-register-donation-decision-drive-continued-growith-organ-and-tissue-donation

The current position in Australia is that the doctors will consult your family about your decision to be an organ donor before donation can take place. Your family can change its mind before your organs and tissue are extracted. It is, therefore, important to discuss your thoughts on organ donation while you are still alive and let your family know that you have noted your thoughts in this manual. With advances in medical science, most organs and tissues can be transplanted or used in some way.

***

Here are my views on organ and tissue donations and which ones I would like or would not like to be donated: _____
_____
_____
_____
_____
_____
_____
_____
_____
_____
_____
_____
_____
_____

My thoughts on donating my cadaver to medical science or for teaching purposes:
_____
_____
_____
_____
_____

Funeral Arrangements

"Do not fear death so much, but rather the inadequate life."
Bertolt Brecht

My Funeral Arrangements

I would prefer to be buried/cremated: _____
My preferred place of burial or where I'd like my ashes scattered or placed: _____
_____

I would prefer a service or memorial to take place at: _____
_____

Preferred religious minister or celebrant: _____
Address: _____
Telephone: _____
I would like the following special arrangements, considerations or type of service for my funeral: _____
_____
_____

Type of coffin or urn: _____
Flowers: _____

Music: _____
_____

Readings: _____
_____

Pall bearers: _____
_____

My headstone: _____
_____
_____

I have made pre-paid funeral arrangements with the following funeral directors or funeral home: _____
Address: _____
Telephone: _____
Documents relating to my pre-paid funeral are located at: _____
Receipt or policy number: _____

Funeral Cover Insurance

I have the following insurance cover relating to funeral expenses:

Insurer: _____
Address: _____
Telephone: _____
Documents relating to my funeral cover are located at: _____
Receipt or policy number: _____

Important note: *you should notify your family if you have pre-paid for your funeral or funeral insurance so as to avoid them paying another funeral home, or not claiming on your policy.*

If I die overseas

"I am ready to meet my Maker. Whether my Maker is prepared for the great ordeal of meeting me is another matter."
- Sir Winston Churchill

In the event that I die overseas I would like the following arrangements to be made: _____
_____
_____
_____

My Obituary

"Everybody dies, but great souls resurrect in our memories."
Michael Bassey Johnson

I would like my obituary published in: _____

Here are a few thoughts on what my obituary may say: _____
_____
_____
_____
_____
_____

My Eulogy

"Did I hear that right? Did someone say ice cream? It's an odd thing to say in the middle of a eulogy, but hell yes, I could go for some ice cream. We could take a break, because it's not like this guy won't still be dead in a half an hour."
 Jarod Kintz, *A Zebra is the Piano of the Animal Kingdom*

I would like my eulogy to be delivered by: _____
_____
_____
_____

Message to be Read at my Funeral

I have recorded a message to be played at my funeral. The file can be located at: _
_____
_____
_____
_____

I would also like the following message read out at my funeral or memorial service: _____

_____
_____
_____
_____
_____
_____
_____
_____
_____
_____
_____
_____
_____
_____
_____
_____
_____
_____
_____
_____
_____
_____
_____
_____
_____
_____
_____
_____
_____

Dated: _____

Notifications

People to notify

On my death, I would like the following people notified:

Name	Address	Email Address	Telephone No.

My social clubs – to notify

On my death, I would like the following social clubs and businesses notified, including any organisation in which I have some form of membership (e.g. professional bodies, trade unions, etc.):

Name	Address	Email Address	Telephone No.

Last Will and Testament

A last Will and Testament, or simply Will, is the primary estate planning tool for most people. The document only becomes operable once you die and can be easily altered prior to death.

Your Will establishes who shall finalise your affairs (your executor). Who will look after your children (their guardian) and how your estate will be distributed, as well as any rules governing the powers your executor will have.

A Will deals only with assets in your personal name. Trusts, life insurance benefits, and superannuation are usually not part of your estate (unless paid into your estate through your instructions or lack of a beneficiary). A Will is generally of little value for these resources. A Will can be of value with non-estate resources through the inclusion of an equalisation clause to balance out payments to beneficiaries from outside your estate. For example, if you want your children to benefit equally, and the trustees of your superannuation do not distribute equally, your Will can balance this up regarding what each of your children receives from your estate.

Likewise, if you have loaned money to a beneficiary, your Will can deal with that as an advance to be offset from their inheritance, or even write it off.

Where you own property as a Joint Tenant, the property automatically passes to the surviving joint owner. You may wish to include an equalisation clause to take into account this benefit that has automatically been received. You should draft your Will with this bigger picture in mind.

The Need for a Will

You need a Will if you wish to decide who should receive your money after you die, who should be appointed as executor, and to appoint a guardian for your children. You need a Will if you are an Appointor to a trust and want to transfer this power to another person who can then appoint a new trustee of this trust if that is ever required.

The powers given to your executor, trustee, appointor or guardian are quite extensive and will determine how your affairs are managed, as well as the welfare of your children.

You must have a Will if you wish to establish a protection mechanism, in the form of a Testamentary Trust, to protect a vulnerable or financially irresponsible family member, such as a bankrupt. You can also specify the age at which children will inherit, as it is a widely held belief that most 18-year-olds are not yet financially responsible.

If you die without a Will, your assets will be distributed according to the laws of intestacy in your State. An interested person must make a Court application to show why they should be appointed to administer your estate. There is a potential for conflict where two or more persons wish to be executor, or disagree with a proposed appointment. For example, where an ex-partner, as the parent and guardian of your minor child, seeks appointment as your executor in conflict with your parents.

When to Revise your Will

As a general rule, you should review and revise your Will during any major life changes.

Marriage and *de facto* relationships

If you have a Will and then marry (unless the Will is specifically drafted in contemplation of the marriage), that Will shall be automatically revoked when you marry. However, if your spouse is provided for in your Will, or appointed as executor, trustee or guardian, these provisions remain valid in Victoria and the Northern Territory.

If you have a Will and commence a *de facto* relationship, your Will is not automatically revoked unless you register your relationship (in certain jurisdictions), which is not common practice. However, it may be appropriate for you to provide for your partner, given that they could make a family provision claim against your estate.

Divorce and Separation

On divorce or the revocation of a registered domestic relationship, any reference to your former spouse or partner in your Will is treated as though he or she predeceased you. Therefore, the remaining provisions of your Will still apply. If your Will did not specify who would receive your former spouse's share if they died, then any gift to them will pass to your intestate beneficiaries, being your most proximal living relatives.

The appointment of your former partner as testamentary trustee or appointor is not necessarily revoked by divorce or the deregistration of the relationship.

In Western Australian and Tasmania, your entire Will is revoked on divorce, unless you have provided otherwise.

Separation does not alter the provisions of your Will, nor does the termination of a *de facto* relationship by simply 'breaking up.' It is all the more prudent to redraft your Will in these circumstances.

Births and deaths

If you have a new child (or perhaps a grandchild), ensure that you have provided for them, including guardianship and trustee arrangements. Failing which the Court would make an appointment, at the expense of your estate.

If a beneficiary dies, your Will should provide for someone else to receive their benefit.

Acquisition and disposal of major assets

This is particularly relevant where you have gifted specific assets to someone or granted a life interest or right of occupation.

If your financial position has significantly altered, consider if the division of assets is still fair, particularly if you have made a large gift to someone, who may then be receiving more or less than you intended considering your overall financial position.

Further, you may purchase property with your partner as Joint Tenants, so that on your death your surviving partner will become the sole owner. If this is the case, will you have sufficient assets to provide for other beneficiaries? In addition, will your estate or surviving partner bear the liability of any mortgage over this property?

Periodically

Circumstances change and the person you appointed as executor, trustee or guardian may no longer be appropriate. You may wish to provide for certain people differently depending on their given needs or circumstances, or you may wish to make use of a Testamentary Trust to provide greater protection of the assets.

Validity of a Will

Each State has its own legislation that prescribes the requirements of a valid Will. However, to be valid, the Will generally needs to be in writing, the Will-maker should sign it in the presence of 2 adult witness, who should also sign. The Will should also be dated.

The Courts want to uphold a Will and therefore strict adherence to the various Will-making rules may not be required, if the Court is satisfied that a document was intended to be a Will, and the Will-maker intended to distribute his or her estate in the manner specified. You should, however ensure that you comply with the rules of Will-making specific to your State to avoid any doubt and inconvenience. Bear in mind that the costs of your executor applying to a Court to prove that a document is a valid Will comes out of your estate.

Things to Consider Before Making a Will

We often have financial resources of differing qualities. It should be remembered that you can nominate your estate as a beneficiary to your Super, or your trust as a beneficiary in your Will, but before making any of these decisions, it is advisable to obtain tax advice.

The Gift of Land

If you gift, or *devise* as is the legal term, land to someone, unless you indicate to the contrary, an existing mortgage on the land passes to the beneficiary. If it is your intention that your estate pays off the mortgage, you should specify this.

Legacies and Bequests

It is common for a Will-maker to specify in their Will that each of their beneficiaries will receive a percentage of the estate, and leave it to them and the executors to determine who gets what, or if everything is to be sold and the proceeds divided in the proportions specified in the Will.

The Will-maker can leave specific items, or bequests, to certain people, or a gift of a specified sum of money (a legacy). Bequests and legacies are paid out of the estate first (after the payment of creditors). Thereafter the Will-maker leaves the balance, or residue, of the estate to named beneficiaries in specified portions. It is important to consider that between the time that you make your Will and when you die, your financial circumstances will likely change. If your wealth decreases, your residuary beneficiaries will get less than what you might have envisaged for them and, in some cases, they may get nothing if the legacies and bequests are large.

You should also bear in mind that due to inflation a monetary gift will decrease in value over time. One way to counteract this is to include an inflation adjustment clause, for example in line with CPI inflation measures. Such a clause needs to be carefully worded to avoid uncertainty.

If you leave a specific gift, and you no longer have it at the time of your death, your executor is obliged to obtain that gift for your beneficiary, unless you make it clear that it is not your intention, such as through the inclusion of an Ademption clause which removes this obligation. You may also leave a specific gift to someone, such as a car or shares which you have never had. Your executor will therefore be obliged to obtain that gift for your nominated recipient. This can be a means of investing for your beneficiary after your death, though you cannot control what they do with this gift after they receive it. Your intentions should be clearly specified.

If a beneficiary dies you should specify that this gift is to pass to someone else or to your residuary estate.

Tax and gifts

When drafting your Will, if you gift certain property to someone, there may be a Capital Gains Tax (CGT) liability attached to that gift, or other taxes and duties, for example, gifts to certain charities, non-residents and certain superannuation funds. You should consider who must pay that liability, the receiver of the gift or your estate (and ultimately your residuary beneficiaries) and you would specify who is to pay it in your Will.

There will be various tax implications that your executor must consider and therefore he or she should obtain tax advice before disposing of any estate assets.

Gifts to charities

Many people enjoy giving to charity and often do so in their Will. You should specify clearly which charity is to benefit, as there are often many branches of the same charity or divisions that may use the funds differently.

If the charity ceases to exist at the time of your death, the gift will not necessarily fail. You could specify an alternative, but if you do not, it is possible for your executor to payout to a different charity that closely resembles your initial choice.

As with all gifts, you should consider the tax consequences. If the charity is an exempt entity with deductible gift recipient status, CGT may not apply. If the charity does not have this status CGT may apply and you will need to decide upon whom the liability lies. Should the charity pay the tax or your estate? Before nominating a charity ascertain its deductible gift recipient (DGR) status. You can consult the Australian Charities and Not for Profits Commission website (acnc.gov.au) for links to the various registers of charities with DGR status. A cash gift would not have CGT issues.

It should also be noted that certain charitable gifts are tax deductible when your executor files tax returns for your estate, but not all, depending on the DGR status of the particular charity recipient. If the beneficiaries themselves made the gift, they would receive the deduction. Alternatively, you can express a non-binding wish that your beneficiaries donate to a charity in your name, if they choose to do so.

Gifts to foreign residents

A gift to a foreign resident could have capital gains tax consequences, payable by your estate. You may wish to consider giving a monetary amount to a non-resident which is not associated with a capital gains asset.

Superannuation

When drafting your Will, you should be sure where your Super benefits will go on your passing. If you have a binding nomination, those beneficiaries specified will receive your Super benefits, and the money by-passes your estate. You should therefore draft your Will with this in mind.

It is possible for the Super to be paid into your estate and distributed according to your Will. Often the trustee of your Super fund has a discretion, unless you have a Binding Death Benefits Nomination. The trustee will otherwise look into the circumstances of your dependants and distribute as they deem appropriate. Does your Will take into account any disparity that the beneficiaries may receive if this is the case?

> CONSIDER: Including an equalisation clause in your Will should one of your beneficiaries receive more from your Super than you expected, or had a tax liability attached to the death benefit, or where the beneficiary of the Super agrees to forego a claim to Super as they would be taxed on it and receives a larger share of the estate to equalise. This opens up the possibilities to tax efficient management of your estate. An equalisation clause can also make adjustments due to inflation.

Repayment of loans to beneficiaries

If you have made a loan to a beneficiary during your lifetime, you can specify that this was an advance on their inheritance, or that it should either be repaid or written off by your executor. Your executor is obliged to secure the repayment of all debts due to you and your estate. If you do not deal with this issue, it is a common cause of dispute.

Executors

The role of the executor and trustee

An executor administers your estate after you die. They are also known as your Personal Legal Representative. They must secure all the assets, arrange the funeral, and decide on how the ashes are to be dealt with if appropriate. They must also apply for the grant of probate, pay off all the debts of the deceased and their estate, including tax. The tax liability, along with all other liabilities must be determined by the executor before distribution of the estate. If there are any challenges to the estate the executor must defend them so as to uphold the terms of the Will.

> NOTE: Severe tax rates apply to taxable estates not distributed, or to which no beneficiary is presently entitled to the taxable income, after 3 years.

The trustee deals with the estate after the executor administers it until the assets are ready to be distributed. The trustee must file tax returns, after obtaining a separate tax file number for the estate or trust as relevant. The trustee may be required to pay tax on behalf of certain beneficiaries such as foreign residents. The executor and trustee are usually the same person and on a practical level the roles are merged.

If your executor dies - before probate

If your executor dies before probate has been obtained, or even before you die, then your second choice of executor as specified in your Will can apply, making note that your first choice has passed away, or is unable to undertake the role. The same applies if your first nomination declines to take up the appointment. Therefore, it is important to discuss the executorship with your proposed executor before signing your Will to ensure that they are willing to act on your behalf.

If your executor dies - after probate

If your executor has been appointed in probate and then subsequently dies, the executor of your executor's estate becomes the executor to your estate. For most, this would be an undesirable result. Therefore, the wording of your executor appointment clause must be carefully drafted to avoid this scenario. You should therefore specify that should your first choice be *unable or unwilling to act or continue to act as your executor*, then your second choice is to be appointed.

Who should you choose

Your chosen executor or executors must be over 18 years of age and with full legal capacity.

Frequently a Will-maker will choose a major beneficiary, such as their partner or adult child. This person should be competent and trustworthy.

You can appoint professionals, such as lawyers, accountants or a trust company as your executor. However, before doing so, you should ascertain their charge out rates, and ensure that they are unable to claim both a commission and professional time based fees for the job. In appointing a professional you will be appointing someone with the required skills and who will objectively administer your estate without personal bias. Professionals are under the scrutiny of their regulatory bodies and require annual trust audits. An independent professional is a good choice where there is a lot of family friction or there are no friends or family members who are suitably skilled or trustworthy. You could also appoint a professional so as not to burden a loved one at such a difficult time. Complex estates may also require professional management.

Choosing more than one executor is beneficial as they will likely keep each other in check, such as one professional and a family member. This could prevent your executor misappropriating your assets or mismanaging your estate.

Powers under the Will that you should consider giving your executor

These are some of the powers that you may wish to consider granting your executor. There are others, so it is best to discuss your particular requirements with your lawyer.

1. Powers by law

The legislation in each State varies as to executors' and trustees' powers, though there are significant similarities. These powers encompass a wide range of scenarios which allow the trustee to be effective. It is a good idea to confirm that the powers given by law are to apply, particularly where State law may vary.

2. Receiving payment

If your trustee is expected to manage a trust for a considerable period, or is a professional, you will need to include the power to be paid, failing which they will be unwilling to act. If there is no trustee, a trustee company will be appointed, which by statute, is entitled to charge for their services, so rather pay for your chosen executor than for one you didn't choose.

Your executor is entitled to seek the Court's authorisation for remuneration. The Court decides each application on its merits.

3. To grant loans

This may be useful where your beneficiaries will not receive their inheritance until a much later date, but one of your beneficiaries requires earlier access to the funds. These funds can be advanced in the form a loan, which can be offset or repaid as appropriate.

4. To ensure no hardship to your guardian

Again, if the guardian you wish to appoint to care for your children would suffer some form of financial hardship in doing so, they may be reluctant or unable to take on the role. The inclusion of this provision allows your executors and trustees to advance funds to your guardian, say to extend their house to accommodate your children. This form of allowance can be made by an interest free loan from the trust or other mechanism appropriate in the circumstances. The executor and trustee will need to consider what is in the best interests of the children, as well as the estate and trust.

5. To sell property

Some people are reluctant to allow the executor or trustee to sell the family home. However, circumstances may necessitate it. If there is adequate reason to do so, and the trustee is unable to sell by virtue of the trust deed, then he or she will need to apply to Court for permission to sell the asset, at the estate's expense. Of course each case is different and the overall extent of the estate or trust will determine if this power is reasonable.

6. Power of appropriation

This is a power to give a beneficiary an asset instead of the amount in money as directed in the Will. The benefit in doing so means that the executor will not be required to sell an asset to meet the legacy obligation.

This is useful where the market may be volatile or where the estate would incur a CGT liability on the sale of the asset. If the asset is given rather than sold, no CGT will be payable (though the beneficiary may have a CGT liability if they later sell).

7. Authorised investments

If you direct your executor and trustee to invest in a certain class of assets only, you should be aware that any assets in your estate and/or trust that are not of this class must be disposed of and converted into the authorised class of investment. Care should be taken in making such a direction, as this could lead to a CGT liability when converting the asset to the authorised class of investment, as well as other transactional expenses such as brokerage or agent's commission. You may wish to specify that the rule applies to new investments only, but you should be clear.

8. Estate expenses

Tax, creditors funeral and estate expenses are paid out of the estate before any beneficiary. When deciding on specific gifts keep in mind these possible expenses, and what assets must be sold to meet them. If you specify the recipient of each asset and there are expenses to be paid, which asset will be sold and therefore which beneficiary may miss out? More likely, each of your beneficiaries may need to pay into the estate if they wish to keep their gift.

9. Receiving under the Will

An executor may receive gifts under your Will. The executor does have an obligation to your estate and cannot unduly benefit from your estate, such as selling an asset to themselves under market value.

***

My Executors

Include the contact details of your executors and cross out those that no longer apply.

Name: _____
Address: _____
Telephone: _____
Email Address: _____

Name: _____
Address: _____
Telephone: _____
Email Address: _____

Name: _____
Address: _____
Telephone: _____
Email Address: _____

Name: _____
Address: _____
Telephone: _____
Email Address: _____

Name: _____
Address: _____
Telephone: _____
Email Address: _____

Challenges to a Will

A Will, or its provisions can be challenged on a number of grounds:

1. The purported Will-maker did not intend to make a Will.

A document that on its surface may appear to be a Will, but was not intended as such, could be disregarded. However, proving this fact can be very difficult. For this reason, you should keep this manual up to date and ensure that you don't sign anything that has the vague appearance of a Will, unless intended.

2. The Will-maker lacked legal capacity to make a Will.

A person without legal capacity, i.e. the understanding of the consequences of their actions, cannot make a Will. A common example is due to dementia or intellectual incapacity. A person may suffer from say Alzheimer's but have lucid moments from time to time. In this case a signed certificate by a medical practitioner to prove that, at the moment the Will was signed, the Will-maker had capacity, would save a Will from being overturned. If your memory is starting to fade and you believe certain family members may be displeased by your Will, you should obtain such a medical certificate when you execute a new Will.

Everything is not lost when a person becomes incapacitated, as an interested person can apply to the Court asking it to approve a statutory Will, which on the evidence the Court would have to be satisfied was the likely Will that this person would have made.

3. The Will-maker signed the Will under duress or undue influence.

If a Will-maker was forced to sign a Will, it will not be upheld. Unfortunately, such pressure is extremely hard to prove, as there are usually no witnesses. This is a common issue in elder abuse, particularly when an elderly person is on their own.

The contents of this manual may be illustrative or used in evidence to sway a Court that the Will may have been signed under duress.

4. The Will-maker failed to adequately provide for someone they had a moral duty to provide for.

This is the most common ground upon which a Will is challenged and a claim is made against an estate. Technically the validity of the Will is not challenged, just its lack of provision.

Each State has its own legislation, but in general a spouse or domestic partner (including dependant former spouse or one who could have made a family law claim), a child (including dependant step-child), dependant grandchild, and dependant parents can make a claim. Each State has its limitations to claims brought by members of these various classes, and therefore you should consult with a lawyer if you have specific concerns about someone in one of these classes of individuals who might make a claim. In the ACT, NSW and in Victoria a person who is in a close personal relationship, or was a registered caring partner with the deceased, may also claim.

It is possible that where someone who would be eligible to make a claim against your estates dies, that their surviving spouse could also make a claim against your estate, in certain circumstances. An example could be your deceased child's partner.

Often a claimant takes a free shot at an estate as the Courts are reluctant to award costs against such claimants. Your estate may bear the full legal costs of both parties to the dispute (the claimant and your executor), which can be substantial. This is a major weakness in this area of law.

Unfortunately, there is no formula to ascertain the likelihood of a successful claim. Factors such as the needs of all beneficiaries and claimants, the size of the estate and the nature of the relationship are all considered.

Measures of Protection to a Claim Against your Estate

1. **Binding Financial Agreement.** The best way to prevent a claim by a current or former partner, is to enter into a Binding Financial Agreement, particularly if it is

your desire that your children (perhaps from a former relationship) receive everything.

2. **Binding Death Benefits Nomination.** Binding Death Benefit Nominations (BDBN) with respect to Super fund and life insurance payments do not form part of your estate and therefore are quarantined from a claim. In NSW, however, the Court may look into any strategy used to avoid a legitimate responsibility to another.

3. **Transfer of title.** If you own property as Joint Tenants (rather than Tenants in Common) that property will automatically bypass your estate and full ownership passes to the surviving Joint Tenant immediately on your death, which can be a useful mechanism. Further, transferring property to another person, say a spouse, on the basis of love and affection, usually does not attract stamp duty and therefore may be feasible during your lifetime. However, this does not protect the asset from the joint owner's creditors or family law claims. There could also be CGT consequences.

4. **Trusts.** Placing assets in a trust, would defeat claims brought against your estate but not necessarily so with a claim by a spouse or partner, under family law.

5. **Lifetime gifts.** You could also give your property to your intended beneficiary before you die, though this could be overturned if your estate is insolvent. But if this person dies before you, you have no control over where the asset thereafter passes.

6. **Deed of Family Arrangement.** You could enter into a Deed of Family Arrangement with all of your potential claimants against your estate, even during your lifetime, wherein they undertake not to challenge your Will or estate. Such a deed would require Court approval.

Long Term Relationships (not *De Facto*)

A number of challenges to a Will arise from people claiming to have been in a *de facto* with the deceased. It is important to know the factors that define a relationship as *de facto* as it may be relevant in legal proceedings brought against you or your estate.

You should seek legal advice to obtain clarity on your relationship and to ascertain whether a Binding Financial Agreement is appropriate for you to protect your assets should you die or terminate that relationship. Alternatively, you could obtain advice from an estate planner or asset protection consultant, who may be able to offer you some advice. However, a Court may look behind such measures in family law proceedings to decide a fair outcome.

The information in this book is of a general nature, without reference to your particular circumstances, and is not to be taken as legal advice. The law is evolving and amendments to legislation or its interpretation by the Courts occur over time.

A *de facto* relationship is one between two persons who are not legally married and are not related (by family) and 'having regard to all the circumstances of their relationship, they have a relationship as a couple living together on a genuine domestic basis.'[3] The *Family Law Act* outlines the relevant circumstances that will be considered by the Court in deciding if the parties were living together on a genuine domestic basis, namely:

"(a) the duration of the relationship;
(b) the nature and extent of their common residence;
(c) whether a sexual relationship exists;
(d) the degree of financial dependence or interdependence, and any arrangements for financial support between them;
(e) the ownership, use, and acquisition of their property;
(f) the degree of mutual commitment to a shared life;
(g) whether the relationship is or was registered under the prescribed law of a State or territory as a prescribed kind or relationship;

---

[3] S4AA(1) of the Family Law Act 1975 (Cth)

(h) the care and support of children;
(i) the reputation and public aspect of the relationship."[4]

The Courts may also look at other factors such as who performs the household duties, and who has raised the children[5]. The Court does not give equal weight to each of these factors, nor does each factor need to be satisfied. For example, a relationship may not be sexual but could still be classified as *de facto*. Also, State law varies as to the factors taken into consideration. Therefore, you should obtain legal advice specific to your State and situation.

Usually, you must have lived together for at least two years. However, if you have children together, a shorter period of cohabitation may suffice.

If your relationship is or was not *de facto*, but the other party disagrees, it would be wise to address each of the factors above in a Statutory Declaration. The declaration is submitted to Court in the event of a claim against your estate by this person, or as a record of your view on your relationship at the time of the declaration. The template included at the end of this book is for this purpose. Remember, you should periodically update this Statutory Declaration, giving reasons for your belief, so that the information remains valid and beneficial.

Where to Store your Will

The easiest way for someone who is disgruntled by your Will to derail your intentions is to simply destroy it. This is unlawful, but proving the destruction of the Will is difficult. If a Will has been destroyed, but a copy found, it is possible for the executor to obtain probate on it if the Court is satisfied that it is a true copy.

In keeping your Will safe, consider placing it in the safe custody of the legal practitioner who drafted it, or it could be filed in the Supreme Court of the State in which you live. When applying for probate, your executor is obliged to sign an affidavit stating that he or she has searched the Court records for your Will so

---

[4] S4AA(2) of the Family Law Act 1975 (Cth)
[5] D v McA (1986) DFC

that probate is not sought on an earlier revoked Will, or on the basis of no Will being located at all.

Alterations to Your Will

You may alter your Will by one of the following methods:

- **Execute a new Will -** This is the most common and best method of changing your Will, particularly when the Will is digitally saved;
- **Crossing out or adding text to the original Will -** The alterations must be signed by the Will-maker and the two witnesses;
- **Executing a codicil -** This addendum specifies which clauses of the original Will are to change, and how. This must be signed and dated by the Will-maker and two witnesses, who need not have witnessed the signing of the Will itself. A codicil can become separated from the Will and therefore is not the best option.

Mutual Wills

Some couples decide to execute Mutual Wills, as well as a deed to execute Mutual Wills, wherein they agree not to alter their Wills without the consent of the other, and where the terms of one Will mirrors the other. Often they agree to leave everything to the surviving spouse and then their children. In doing this they would be aiming to ensure that should the surviving spouse remarry, then the agreed terms shall continue. This ensures that the couple's children inherit rather than the second spouse and his or her family to the exclusion of the Will-makers' children.

Unfortunately, a Mutual Will may not defeat a claim by the second surviving spouse or *de facto* under family provision legislation. It is the duty of a Will-maker to provide for his or her dependants, failing which the Court can alter the Will to make such provision. It would also require one of the primary couple's beneficiaries to challenge any new Will made in contravention of the deed, which could be a costly endeavour.

International Wills and Assets

If you have assets in more than one country, you may wish to draft separate Wills for each country as a Will drafted in one country may not be valid in another. However, as a general principle of law, if a Will is valid in the country in which it is executed, it is most often upheld in other places. If you draft more than one Will, ensure that one Will does not revoke the other and be very clear as to which jurisdiction it applies. Legal advice is a must in these circumstances.

The alternative to multiple Wills is the International Will. There are specific rules relating to the execution of such a Will, for example it must be signed before an authorised witness, such as a notary. International Wills are recognised in most countries. Please check that they are recognised in the country in which you hold assets.

Revocation of a Will

You can revoke your Will by:
1. Executing a new Will with a clause revoking the prior Will;
2. Destroying the Will with the intention of revoking it;
3. Directing someone else to destroy it in your presence with the intention of revoking it;
4. By written Deed of Revocation noting that your Will of a certain date is revoked. This must be signed by the Will-maker in the presence of two adult witnesses.

Deed of Family Arrangement

A Deed of Family Arrangement is a document whereby the beneficiaries to a Will agree to a redistribution of an estate, thereby effectively altering the provisions of the Will.

Though not common, such a deed could be entered into during your life time so that the beneficiaries of your Will can release any claim to your estate other than as provided for in your Will. Such a deed would need to be approved by Court and each jurisdiction differs in this regard. Therefore, you should consult with a solicitor to establish whether this is a viable solution to preventing someone from making a claim against your estate. Such a deed would only be concluded by the class of person eligible to make a claim against your estate, such as a *de facto* or child.

Dying Without a Will

If you do not have a Will, or your Will does not provide for the distribution of all of your assets, you are said to have died intestate or partially intestate. In this case the law of the State in which you live permanently and the State in which your assets are located shall determine who gets your assets. Each State is different. In some States, your spouse or partner will receive your entire estate, in others he or she may receive a share of your estate and your children the rest. Also, the provisions vary depending on whether or not the spouse is the parent of the deceased's children. There are varying provisions should you die legally married and have a *de facto* partner.

There are also variations as to the definition of domestic partner. Usually the term requires a domestic relationship with the deceased for at least two years prior to death. However, South Australian legislation requires a relationship spanning five of the last six years prior to death.

If you have no partner or children, your assets would generally pass to your parents, or your siblings and possibly their children. Failing the existence of anyone in these categories, grandparents are then next in line and thereafter aunts and uncles and possibly their children.

As you can see there are a lot of variables, therefore it is best to execute a Will. Given that you have bought this book, I would expect that this is something that you would be inclined to do. Also having a Will can prevent dispute between your potential beneficiaries in the future, with the estate often bearing the legal costs.

My Will

Date: _____ Will or Codicil? _____
Held at: _____
Electronic copy saved on my computer as: _____
If revoked, where is it _____

Date: _____ Will or Codicil? _____
Held at: _____
Electronic copy saved on my computer as: _____
If revoked, where is it _____

Date: _____ Will or Codicil? _____
Held at: _____
Electronic copy saved on my computer as: _____
If revoked, where is it _____

Date: _____ Will or Codicil? _____
Held at: _____
Electronic copy saved on my computer as: _____
If revoked, where is it _____

Notes on Why I Drafted my Will as I Did

Your beneficiaries may wonder why you drafted your Will as you did. They may be inclined to challenge your Will believing that you may have been coerced into signing it, or didn't know what you were doing. And some may look for meaning in the gifts that you gave.

Further if you have excluded someone who might expect that you would provide for them, such as a *de facto* or child, you might wish to offer up your reasoning.

The following information relates to my Will dated _____

I decided that the age that someone should receive a benefit under my Will was _____ years because _____
_____
_____
_____

I left the specific gift items that I did because _____
_____
_____
_____
_____
_____

I decided not to leave specific gift items to my beneficiaries because _____
_____
_____
_____
_____
_____

I excluded _____ from my Will because _____
_____
_____
_____
_____
_____
_____
_____

I did not distribute my estate equally as you may have expected because _____
_____
_____
_____
_____

The reason I chose _____ as my executor is because _____

_____
_____

The reason I chose _____ as the guardian of my children is because _____
_____
_____
_____
_____

Other reasons: _____
_____
_____
_____
_____
_____
_____

Further Notes on Why I Re-drafted my Will

The following information relates to my Will dated _____
I decided that the age that someone should receive a benefit under my Will was _____ years because _____
_____

I left the specific gift items that I did because _____
_____
_____
_____
_____

I decided not to leave specific gift items to my beneficiaries because _____
_____
_____

_____
_____
_____
_____
_____

I excluded _____ from my Will because _____
_____
_____
_____
_____
_____
_____

I did not distribute my estate equally as you may have expected because _____
_____
_____
_____
_____

The reason I chose _____ as my executor is because _____
_____
_____

The reason I chose _____ as the guardian of my children is because _____
_____
_____

Other reasons: _____
_____
_____
_____

Probate Guide

When planning your estate, it is important to consider the process of probate and estate administration.

After your death, your executor must usually do as follows:

1. Attend to funeral arrangements;
2. Secure all of your assets;
3. Locate your original Will;
4. Consult a solicitor for legal advice on applying for probate;
5. Advertise their intention to apply for probate;
6. Draft Court papers, being the application, executor's affidavit, inventory of assets, parchment and exhibits to be attached, such as the death certificate and affidavit of searches;
7. Check Court registers for Wills or applications lodged, and file an affidavit confirming that they have done so;
8. Lodge the application and pay Court fees;
9. Attend to requisitions by the Court requiring clarification or further information;
10. Grant of probate is obtained;
11. Administer the estate by securing all the assets, paying the bills, etc.;
12. Liaise with beneficiaries and locate them;
13. Attend to your place of residence;
14. Attend to your household and personal items;
15. Notify all authorities and all interested parties of their appointment;
16. Protect and insure estate assets;
17. Draft Application of Personal Representative (APR) with land titles office to transfer your property into their name in their capacity as executor;
18. Transfer property to surviving Joint Tenant;
19. Draft and advertise a Notice to Creditors;
20. Wait at least 6 months from date of probate to distribute, but no later than 12 months after;
21. Deal with accounts and accounting;

22. Continue management of estate as trustee;
23. File tax returns;
24. Defend estate from claims;
25. Liaise with guardians of children for ongoing financial support;
26. Maintain assets held in trust;
27. Make reasonable investment decisions;
28. Seek financial and tax advice as to the proper administration of the estate.

Each estate is different and therefore the administration of your estate may differ.

Is your nominated executor up for the task? Your executor can appoint a solicitor to perform many of these tasks, at the expense of your estate. You can also utilise this manual to make each of these steps easier for your executor.

Suggestions to Beneficiaries of my Estate on How to Manage Their Inheritance

Your suggestions can relate to tax efficiency in superannuation death benefits, or lump sum vs pension payments. You may wish to suggest an investment strategy, or perhaps an Estate Proceeds Trust. Please refer to the various sections in this book when considering your options.

My suggestions

Note that this is not intended to be a testamentary direction to my executors regarding the dealings of my assets. I am merely suggesting investment possibilities for my executor and beneficiaries.

Asset/beneficiary: _____
Suggestion: _____
_____
_____

Asset/beneficiary: _____
Suggestion: _____
_____
_____

Asset/beneficiary: _____
Suggestion: _____
_____
_____

Asset/beneficiary: _____
Suggestion: _____
_____
_____

Others for Whom I Care

There will be people who depend on you. Perhaps you just help them out from time to time, or visit a lonely aged person regularly. You may have even been appointed this person's guardian, or know that there are people out there who would be lost without you, and would like someone else to help out as you do.

Name: _____
Contact details: _____
_____
_____

Care that I've been providing: _____
_____
_____

Name: _____
Contact details: _____
_____
_____

Care that I've been providing: _____
_____
_____

Name: _____
Contact details: _____
_____
_____

Care that I've been providing: _____
_____
_____

Pets

Your furry, feathered or scaled companions will miss you when you're gone and will be in need of care. Leave your wishes and instructions for the precious creatures in your life.

Name of pet: _____
Breed/species: _____
Name and address of vet: _____
Location of vet's certificate: _____
Registered? _____
Any special concerns or considerations: _____
_____
_____

My wishes: _____
_____

Name of pet: _____
Breed/species: _____
Name and address of vet: _____
Location of vet's certificate: _____
Registered? _____
Any special concerns or considerations: _____
_____

My wishes: _____
_____

Name of pet: _____
Breed/species: _____
Name and address of vet: _____
Location of vet's certificate: _____

Registered? _____
Any special concerns or considerations: _____
_____
_____

My wishes: _____
_____

Name of pet: _____
Breed/species: _____
Name and address of vet: _____
Location of vet's certificate: _____
Registered? _____
Any special concerns or considerations: _____
_____
_____

My wishes: _____
_____

Name of pet: _____
Breed/species: _____
Name and address of vet: _____
Location of vet's certificate: _____
Registered? _____
Any special concerns or considerations: _____
_____
_____

My wishes: _____
_____

Charities I Support.

I support the following charities. I may have direct debits from my account, which will need to be cancelled. Some people may wish to send donations to these charities, in lieu of flowers at my funeral.

Charity: _____
Contact details: _____
Nature of support given: _____
_____

Charity: _____
Contact details: _____
Nature of support given: _____
_____

Charity: _____
Contact details: _____
Nature of support given: _____
_____

Charity: _____
Contact details: _____
Nature of support given: _____
_____

Charity: _____
Contact details: _____
Nature of support given: _____
_____

6
MESSAGES
Letters to Loved Ones

You may wish to take this opportunity to leave a comforting letter to your loved ones. Here are a few prompts to get you going.

I love you because…
The qualities that you possessed…
You have made my life better by …
My fondest memory of you is…
Please forgive…
I forgive …
My hopes for you in the future are…
Please take my advice that …
I need to tell you…
Please look after…
My reasons for…
If I could do one thing all over again, it would be…
I was happiest when…

I have written the following letters to my loved ones:

Date	To Whom	Instructions for delivering the letter

These letters are kept: _____

_____

(suggestion: keep them at the back of this manual)

Letters for Forgiveness

We've all done things that we are not proud of, or wronged someone. Now is the time and the place to put those wrongs to rights. Of course, there's no reason to wait until you're gone before you ask for forgiveness, but sometimes there's something that stops us doing so in the here and now.

Here is a template for such a letter, though of course you may write it any way you choose.

I am sorry that I …
I know you must have felt …
My reasons for doing what I did are that …
I wish …
In doing what I did I feel …
I further wish to say to you …

I have written the following letter asking for forgiveness:

Date	To Whom	Instructions for delivering the letter

These letters are kept: _____

(suggestion: keep them at the back of this manual)

Letter to the Future Step-parent of my Children

For many of us the thought of leaving our children terrifies us and the thought of being replaced by someone else may frighten us even more. The job of a parent is for life, not just until your child reaches the age of 18. The role may change over time, but there will only ever be one you.

What follows is a prompt to get you started should you wish to write a letter to your child's possible future or current step-parent.

Dear Step-parent,
I hope that you can understand how hard it is for me to write this letter. I hope you can understand and respect the unique role that I have in my child's life. I hope that you will do the right thing and respect my memory and support my child. I understand that you will have your own unique role to play. I know that the role of a step-parent can be challenging and I also want my child to know that there is room enough for both of us in his or her life, and in so doing I hope that you will love my child.
    I would also like to say …
    Something you should be aware of is …
    My child's relationship with me has been …
    My child's relationship with his/her other parent has been …
    Things that make my child happy …
    Things that upset my child …
    My child is frightened by …
    My child gets angry when …
    Thank you for taking the time to read this and I hope you come to love my child.
Yours sincerely,

This letter is kept: _____
_____
(suggestion: keep it at the back of this manual)

Guardians of my Children

A guardian is someone appointed, either in your Will or by a Court, to look after a child (or any person with an incapacity) when neither parent is able.

If the child has a disability, the guardianship will remain in place for as long as required. There are various State agencies which will petition the Court for guardianship over a child if there are no appropriate relatives.

A guardian is responsible for the day to day care of the child and has custody of him or her. Guardians make all medical and lifestyle decisions for the child to the same extent as a parent. The guardian does not have control over the assets in your estate that are left for your child; it is the executor and trustee who manage these funds on behalf of the child until the child reaches the appropriate age. The guardian will usually request funds from the estate for the support of the child. You can make particular provision for these expenses in your Will.

Some information that you may wish to leave for them

You cannot dictate to the guardian how they should raise your child, but you can provide your views.

- **Religious education and worship**: How would you like your guardian to maintain or advance your views on religion for your child.

- **Education**: How would you like your child supported in his or her education?

- **Discipline and responsibility**: What are your views on this issue?

- **Pocket money**: Should this be a matter of right or should the child earn it?

- **Chores**: Everyone needs to contribute to the running of the household in which they live, but to what extent? What have been your expectations of your child?

- **Exercise**: What views on exercise have you been trying to instil in your child?

- **Extramural activities**: Some parents insist that their child is heavily involved in extramural activities, others not so much. What are your thoughts?

- **Dating**: This is another issue around which some family rules relate. Some parents are conservative and others less so.

- **University**: You should specify the extent to which your estate may financially provide for fees in your Will. You can also give your input on the matter here.

- **Part-time employment**: Do you believe that a child should obtain some form of employment once they are old enough to do so?

- **Babysitters**: Who do you employ?

- **Choice of primary or high school**: Private or public, religious or secular. What is right for your child? Have you put your child's name down somewhere?

- **Tutors**: Who do you employ?

- **Sports**: Your thoughts?

- **Other considerations**: Any other issues that are important.

- **Gifts:** Some gifts that you would like given on certain special occasions.

My Notes to my Guardians

In the event of my death I understand that I should appoint a guardian for my minor children in my Will. If I should die before my children have reached adulthood, I would like the following to be appointed guardian, in order of preference:

Name: _____ Date of nomination: _____
Address: _____
Telephone: _____
Relationship to me: _____

Name: _____ Date of nomination: _____
Address: _____
Telephone: _____
Relationship to me: _____

Name: _____ Date of nomination: _____
Address: _____
Telephone: _____
Relationship to me: _____

Here are a few things I would like the guardian to know. I hope that the guardian of my child/ren will take these thoughts into consideration when raising my child, as they are important to me:

Religious education and worship: _____
_____
_____

Education: _____
_____
_____

Discipline and responsibility: _____
_____

Pocket money: _____
_____

Chores: _____
_____

Exercise: _____
_____

Extramural activities: _____
_____

Dating: _____
_____

University: _____
_____

Part time employment: _____
_____

Babysitters: _____
_____

Choice of primary school: _____
_____

Choice of high school: _____
_____

Tutors: _____

_____
_____
_____
Sports: _____
_____
_____
Other considerations: _____
_____
_____
_____

I would like you to give the following gifts from me on the occasions noted as a way of showing my love (birthday, wedding, graduation, etc.)

Person	Gift	Occasion	Reason

7

TEMPLATES

Will Kit

Instructions

It is advisable for you to consult a lawyer to draft and assist you in executing your Will. However, if you choose not to see a lawyer, you have the option of completing the enclosed Will Kit and executing it as your last Will. Your circumstances or the manner in which you would like to distribute your assets once you die may be more complicated than this simple Will Kit allows. This Will Kit is intended for fairly ordinary and uncomplicated estates. Please consult a lawyer if your circumstances warrant a more complicated or detailed Will, or if you are unsure of what to write.

    The purpose of a Will is to nominate those who will receive a specified asset or a portion of your estate. It will also appoint an executor to administer your estate, pay off the debts and distribute the assets to your beneficiaries. You can also appoint a guardian to take care of any of your children who are under the age of 18.

    You will need to fill in all the details before you sign. You will need two witnesses who are over the age of 18 years and of full legal and mental capacity (i.e. they fully understand that they are witnessing the execution of a Will). Your witnesses do not need to read your Will or know the details of your intentions. You must sign and date the Will in the presence of the two witnesses, who must then also sign in the space provided, and fill in their details. Some States have a rule that a witness cannot be a beneficiary in the Will. Therefore, your witnesses should not be any of your beneficiaries. Sometimes, even in jurisdictions where a witness can inherit, such as Victoria, the fact that a witness is a beneficiary may lead to questions surrounding undue influence to obtain a benefit from your Will. Choose independent witnesses.

If you need to amend your Will (before it is signed), you and your witnesses must initial the changes. You must not add text to a Will after it has been signed. If you change your mind, you should revoke the Will by executing a new one.

You can make specific gifts to named persons (either in money or assets) which will be allocated before any residuary gifts (i.e. those getting the balance of your estate). You will then need to decide who gets whatever is left after you have given the specific gifts and in what proportion. You do not need to give specific gifts. It is quite common to share your estate out equally among your children for example.

An example and further explanation of each of the clauses in the Will Kit is given below. Please cross reference these explanations with the draft Will Kit provided.

Clause 1. This is a standard clause. It may not be appropriate if you have a Will in another country which you wish to remain valid. Please consult with a lawyer, so you don't accidently revoke it.

Clause 2. This is a standard executor appointment clause, you should make an alternative appointment, just in case.

Clause 3. This is a standard guardian appointment clause. Again you should make an alternative appointment, just in case.

Clause 4. Examples of Gifts

I give the following gifts:

Recipient (full name)	Gift
Jane Elizabeth Smith	$1,000.00
William Smith	My antique Bavarian Cuckoo Clock
Amy Victoria Smith	My Stamp Collection
Gillian Smith	All of my gold jewellery and $3,000.00

You should cross through any blank spaces to ensure that no further information can be inserted without your knowledge.

Clause 5 of the Will means that if you no longer own the cuckoo clock at the time of your death, then William would not receive any gifts under this clause. If you delete clause 5, your executor might be obliged to search for your clock to get it for William.

Clause 6 deals with how the remainder of your estate should be distributed.

Examples:

'I leave the residue of my estate to my husband, Roger Smith. If my husband should die before me, then I give the residue of my estate to my children, Belinda Smith, Declan Smith and Amy Victoria Smith in equal shares.'

'I leave the balance of my estate, in equal shares, to the survivors of Roger Smith, Belinda Smith, Declan Smith and Amy Victoria Smith.' **This means that your estate will be divided equally among these people but only so long as they outlive you. (Clause 8 in the template will therefore not apply.)**

'I give the balance of my estate as follows: 50% to Roger Smith, 10% to Belinda Smith, 25% to Declan Smith and 15% to Amy Victoria Smith. Provided that should any of these beneficiaries die before me or simultaneously with me, then that person's share shall be divided amongst the survivors in proportion to their share.' **(Again clause 7 in the template would not apply.)**

'I leave the balance of my estate to be divided equally between Roger Smith, provided he survives me, and the Royal Dogs Home of Victoria or such similar charity that rescues and rehomes dogs that may exist if the Royal Dogs Home of Victoria is no longer in existence.'

A child can inherit once they reach 18 years of age. **Clause 7** in the template is included should you wish to delay a young person receiving his or her inheritance until they are a little older and possibly more responsible. The executor will need to continue to look after the gifts given to a child until they reach the nominated age. It is, therefore, advisable not to specify too old an age, as this will become onerous for the executor.

With the inclusion of **Clause 8** in the template, if you name someone to receive a gift and they have already died, that gift will pass to their children, provided they have a child. If that person does not have a child, the gift will pass to the remaining residuary beneficiaries. Similarly, if you exclude this clause (by crossing it out and you and the witnesses initialling the change or by including the provision: 'provided they survive me'), then that gift or share of the estate will fall to the remainder, if the named beneficiary dies before you.

Checklist:

[ ] I have used my full name and current residential address.
[ ] I have used my executors' full names and their addresses.
[ ] I have appointed a guardian who has already agreed to act as my guardian.
[ ] I have used everyone's full names.
[ ] I have described the gifts in detail so that there can be no doubt about my intentions.
[ ] I have specified who will receive the remainder of my estate after distribution of the specific gifts.
[ ] I have specified what will happen if my residuary beneficiaries should die before receiving their inheritance.
[ ] I have specified the age at which young beneficiaries will inherit.

[ ] I have dated the Will.
[ ] I completed the Will before signing it.
[ ] I have crossed out any blank spaces.
[ ] The witnesses and I were all together when we each signed.
[ ] The witnesses and I initialled at the bottom of the first page and any alterations.
[ ] The witnesses and I signed using the same pen.
[ ] The witnesses filled in their full name, occupation, address and telephone number in the space provided.
[ ] I have crossed out any paragraphs that I wish to remove and the witnesses and I have initialled next to the changes.

The Will contained in the following pages may be completed and cut out of this manual and placed into safe keeping where your executor can find it.

Last Will And Testament

This WILL is made by me_____ (full name) of _____ (address) in the State of _____ (State).

1. I hereby revoke all previous Wills and Testamentary acts.
2. (a) I appoint_____(name) of _____ (address) as my Executor and Trustee.

    (b) If the abovementioned person is unable or unwilling to act or continue to act as my Executor and Trustee then I appoint _____ (name) of _____(address) as my Executor and Trustee.
3. (a) I appoint _____(name) of _____ (address) as Guardian to any child of mine who is younger than 18 years at the time of my death.

    (b) If the abovementioned person is unable or unwilling to act or continue to act as my Guardian then I appoint _____ (name) of _____ (address) instead.
4. I give the following gifts:

Recipient (full name)	Gift

5. Any gift made in this Will is subject to my retaining an interest in the property as at the time of my death.
6. I give the residue of my estate, after due payment of all outstanding debts by my Executor, to: _____

_____
_____
_____
_____
_____
_____
_____

7. I direct that each beneficiary to my Estate shall be entitled to their gift or share on reaching the age of _____ years (age upon which to inherit).
8. If a beneficiary referred to in this Will has already died or does not survive me or dies before attaining a vested interest, leaving children who survive me, then those children take equally the share of any disposition which their parent would otherwise have taken, unless expressly provided otherwise.

Dated _____

The Will-maker signed in the presence of both of us, and we attested to the Will-} maker's signature in their presence and of} each other.

_____
Signature of Will-maker

Witness 1 sign here: Witness 2 sign here:

_____   _____

Full name: Full name:
Occupation: Occupation:
Address: Address:

Phone: Phone:

Statutory Declaration Template

For use regarding *de facto* relationships, or in the case of where you have excluded someone from your Will who may be entitled to receive a share of your estate, by virtue of your obligations to them, but who you have excluded for clear and valid reasons, which should be specified.

You should address each point that you wish to make in a separate numbered paragraph.

The following professionals may witness a statutory declaration, in terms of the Statutory Declarations Regulations 1993. For a full list of appropriate witnesses, please consult the Regulations.

Bank manager
School principal
Notary public
Councillor of a municipality
Justice of the peace
Pharmacist
Barrister
Member of the police force
Solicitor
Doctor
Dentist
Veterinary surgeon
Full-time teacher

Please refer to www.the-life-manual.com for templates specific to your State.

STATUTORY DECLARATION

I, _____ (full name), of _____
(address), in the State of _____, _____
(occupation) do solemnly and sincerely make the following declaration under the *Statutory Declarations Legislation* applicable in my State:

_____
_____
_____
_____
_____
_____
_____
_____
_____
_____
_____
_____
_____
_____
_____
_____
_____
_____
_____
_____
_____
_____
_____
_____
_____

_____I understand that a person who intentionally makes a false statement in a statutory declaration is guilty of an offence under section 11 of the *Statutory Declarations Act 1959*, and I believe that the statements in this declaration are true in every particular.

DECLARED at _____)
In the State of _____ on)
the ____ day of _____ 20___) _____
Before me: Declarant

Witness
Name_____
Address_____
_____
Qualification_____

NOTES

Use this space should you have further information to add

FINAL WORD

I must reiterate that you should keep the information in this manual safe and you should not disclose any sensitive information that could be abused, such as PIN numbers and passwords.

You may wish to encrypt some of the information so that only a trusted family member or friend will be able to decipher it.

Please register at www.the-life-manual.com to receive updates that may be relevant to you.

Please visit www.the-life-manual.com to download addition copies of documents included in this book or the purchase additional copies of this book.

ABOUT THE AUTHOR

Hazel is a solicitor, admitted to practice law in Victoria, Australia. Before emigrating to Australia she was admitted to practice in Botswana, having read for her law degree in South Africa.

She now runs her own practice dealing primarily in Wills and Estates, as well as family law. She has experience, both personally and professionally, in the issues that arise when dealing with an estate after a loved one passes.

She wrote this book because she believes that we can help those that we love, even in the most difficult of times, after we pass away.

Let's make it easier for the ones we leave behind.